THE BUSINESS ENTERPRISE IN
MODERN INDUSTRIAL SOCIETY

THEMES AND ISSUES IN MODERN
SOCIOLOGY

The Business Enterprise
in
Modern Industrial Society

JOHN CHILD

London Graduate School of Business Studies

COLLIER-MACMILLAN LIMITED LONDON
The Macmillan Company

Collier-Macmillan Limited
10 South Audley Street, London W1

The Macmillan Company,
Collier-Macmillan Canada Ltd, Toronto

Library of Congress Catalogue Card Number: 69-10536

First printing 1969

Printed in Great Britain
by Butler and Tanner Ltd, Frome and London

CONTENTS

PREFACE

The business enterprise has long been a subject of keen interest to sociologists. This interest has today become diversified into many lines of enquiry, and it often impinges on matters which are of concern also to economists and psychologists. Accordingly, an extensive literature on the business enterprise is available. A considerable proportion of this literature is highly specialized in nature, while certain sources adopt a very selective standpoint.

It is therefore as a guide into a complex and contentious field of study that this book is offered. It attempts to review concisely the major issues concerning the role of the business enterprise in contemporary industrial societies, and to assess relevant sociological argument and research. I hope that this book will encourage the reader subsequently to make his own more detailed examination of particular issues which he finds of interest. To this end I have appended a lengthy and selectively annotated bibliography. For those who are already familiar with my theme, this review may prove to be a handy compact source of material and references.

I have incurred several debts of gratitude in producing this book. The editors of this series, Mrs Jean Floud and Mr John Goldthorpe, have given me every advice and encouragement. Mrs Silvia Davies worked wonders in typing from my manuscript. Mrs Judith McQuillan patiently helped me to check the proofs. My wife, Elizabeth, lent a very necessary critical faculty, and suffered the usual deprivations of an author's wife—I hope not in vain.

J.C.

CHAPTER I

The Characteristic Institution
of Modern Industrial Society

Business enterprises as we know them today are part and
parcel of industrialization. Many of the changes which permit
historians to identify the industrial revolution also describe
the development of the business enterprise into its most
characteristic modern form. Resources became increasingly
concentrated under a unified control, the processes of manufacture were technologically integrated into factory systems,
and the number of large firms greatly increased (Ashton,
1948; Pollard, 1965). These developments continue apace
even in contemporary advanced economies. They have already contributed to massive socio-industrial changes since
the late eighteenth century, and they have brought the business enterprise to the forefront of modern social institutions.
Indeed, there are both admirers and critics of the business
enterprise who identify it as the characteristic and leading
institution of modern industrial societies (e.g. Drucker, 1946;
Hacker, 1965a). They argue that the values and modes of
social organization which are amalgamated in the business
enterprise as a social institution today exercise a predominant
influence over people's lives in modern society.

It is not difficult to appreciate the reasons for this view.
The larger business enterprise comprises an enormous concentration of wealth and power. Giant international companies, such as British Petroleum (with around 450 subsidiaries) or Unilever (with several hundred subsidiaries
operating in over 50 countries), have become supra-national
organizations. Their internal decisions may have as much
impact on patterns of trade and international relations as
decisions taken by governments themselves (Kronstein, 1965;

Tugendhat, 1968a). The incomes of the largest contemporary business enterprises exceed those of many nation states. The men in charge of such organizations exercise a correspondingly large influence over the material conditions of individual lives through their decisions on matters such as investment, employment, location, products and prices. Even more than this, it can seriously be argued that business values have, through the mass media and the interpenetration of governmental and business decision making, now secured a dominant influence within the culture-patterns of modern industrial society (Galbraith, 1967).

1 BIG BUSINESS

It is primarily because they have recognized how the large business enterprise is in many ways becoming a power unto itself, that sociologists, economists and other commentators have given most of their attention to 'Big Business'. The notorious remark that 'What is good for General Motors is good for the United States', would not have aroused such passionate misunderstanding if General Motors were not the powerful giant that it is.[1] It has been realized that large business enterprises do pose particularly acute political, social and organizational problems. Many of those in control of larger enterprises have also shared in this realization. They have in the main proved more receptive to investigation, while public companies (normally the larger ones) have also been obliged by law to disclose more information about their activities. Big Business is therefore in the public eye. It plays a leading socio-economic role as the following statistics suggest, and it has been the focus of most of the argument and research reviewed in this book.

The epitome of Big Business, brought alive by writers such as Drucker (1946) and Sloan (1965), is the General Motors Corporation. This is the world's largest privately-owned business enterprise which, leaving aside its many international subsidiaries, had sales of £8,045 million and a capital of £4,339 million in 1967–8. In 1962 it employed over 600,000

---

[1] We are in fact informed by Robert Johnson, General Motors public relations manager, that what the head of his company actually said was, 'I've always thought that what was good for the country was good for General Motors, and vice versa' (Johnson, 1966).

people. In Britain the largest enterprises are nationalized industries such as the Electricity Council and Boards with over £4,000 million capital and almost 240,000 employees during 1967–8; and the Post Office and the National Coal Board, both employing less capital but each with over 400,000 personnel. The largest continental European company during the same period was estimated to be Royal Dutch Petroleum with a capital employed of over £2,400 million (Dill, 1965; *The Times 500*, 1968). Large firms depend upon a large total market, which explains why they have expanded either internationally or through product diversification, or through both together. Thus many large groups can be found operating in a wide range of different industries, a notable example being the British firm Thomas Tilling whose activities include bulk haulage, chain making, steel furniture, motor components, glassware, textiles, building materials, insurance, vehicle distribution and wholesaling! (Dun & Bradstreet, 1967).

While the bulk of business activity in modern industrial societies is now accounted for by larger enterprises, they remain unrepresentative of the total number of firms. In the United Kingdom during 1961, 34·5% of those employed in manufacturing industry worked in establishments employing 1,000 persons or more, although such establishments were only 2·2% of the total (Annual Abstract of Statistics, 1968). Many companies have more than one establishment, and hence large companies account for an even more preponderant share of economic resources. At the end of 1963, as much as 57% of the total net assets of 2,027 companies examined by the Board of Trade were accounted for by the 100 largest companies alone (Stacey, 1966, pp. 24–6).

Large business enterprises play a dominant role in other modern industrial societies. In 1962 the 50 largest United States corporations held over one-third of all manufacturing assets, and the 500 largest held well over two-thirds. In the mid 1950s, 23 corporations provided around 10% of all US manufacturing employment, while in 1960 four corporations accounted for an estimated 22% of all industrial research and development expenditure (Galbraith, 1967, p. 75). France and Germany have experienced marked trends towards industrial concentration—proportionately fewer and larger enterprises in given industries—while other countries, especially Italy and Japan, have experienced an even more rapid development of giant enterprise since the mid-1950s (Stacey, 1966, pp. 19–21). 'Gigantomania', the urge to grow through mergers, has never been more pronounced in European industry than it is today. During 1968 Britain was at the head of the rush with quoted companies spending on mergers nearly three times the annual average for 1959 to 1963, and over eight times the average for 1954 to 1958 (Tugendhat, 1968b).

In capitalist industrial societies, joint stock companies account for a very predominant share of business activity (Allen, 1966, p. 181; Dahrendorf, 1959, p. 42). This is the most common legal form adopted by large business enterprises, though in Britain the nationalized public corporation also plays a major role (Tivey, 1966). At the same time, enterprises in most societies can possess different legal statuses which may vary in suitability according to factors such as company size, potential rate of growth, and availability of capital. The status of British business ranges from self-employment, partnership, private or public joint-stock company, to nationalized public corporation. Each status carries different legal obligations, particularly with regard to public accountability (Ennis, 1967). In communist societies the enterprise takes on yet another legal and organizational identity as an adjunct of state planning bureaucracy, though some private enterprise may be permitted on a very small scale.

2 CONCEPTUAL PROBLEMS

The variety of legal and organizational forms through which business enterprises may operate in different industrial societies suggests correctly that the central concept of 'the business enterprise' is open to ambiguity.

We mentioned earlier that the business enterprise (at least in a collective sense) could be considered as a social institution in that it represented an amalgamation of values and social organization. The distinction between the values subsumed in the notion of business enterprise, which may themselves be expressed by a variety of goals, and an organizational framework is an important one. For it allows us a necessary conceptual flexibility when analysing business enterprises which accords with their empirical diversity. That is, it draws attention to the possibility of differences in business objectives among enterprises which in a technical sense are organized similarly, and equally to the possibility of organizational differences among enterprises pursuing similar business objectives.[2]

As might be expected from these remarks, no single wholly satisfactory definition of the business enterprise is available. Dill (1965) lists many competing formulations. Some definitions stress the goals and motivations of those in charge of business enterprises, such as profit-making. Others stress the contractual and economic nature of the activities and relationships which underlie the operation of such enterprises. Blau and Scott distinguish business organizations as those whose prime beneficiaries are their owners (1963, p. 43). This criterion of prime beneficiary has attracted considerable attention since it enables an apparently clear differentiation to be made between business and other organizations such as 'mutual benefit associations' or 'service organizations'.

Yet even this definition is problematic. The assumption that owners are the prime beneficiaries of business organizations overlooks the debate current in western societies as to whether the primary goal even of privately-owned business is necessarily directed towards the benefit of its legal ownership (see Chapter III below). In a socialist society, where all organizations of any importance are publicly owned, the Blau-Scott criterion does not unambiguously distinguish between business and other organizations. Indeed, characteristics which are often assumed to mark the business enterprise, such as production for profit or the competitive disposal of outputs through a market system, do not necessarily apply outside capitalist societies or even to publicly-owned enterprises within them. The common notion of 'business' is in fact not wholly applicable to socialist societies or to 'socialized' enterprises. On the other hand, some structural features frequently associated with the business enterprise, such as contractual relationships, may also be found in organ-

---

[2] The distinction also permits one to discriminate between business and non-business organizations in terms of their prescribed goals, while at the same time to compare them in terms of their behavioural and structural characteristics. Much comparative work in modern organization theory is in fact following this course (cf. Pugh *et al.*, 1963). We shall in this book use the terms 'business enterprise' and 'business organization' interchangeably, and in fact the conceptual problem relates primarily to the limits which should be imposed on the use of the adjective.

izations performing very different social functions.

In short, we are forced to return to the distinction between values and organization. For the problem of delimiting the business enterprise results from the fact that the values contained in the idea of 'business' do not apply identically throughout all modern industrial societies, while the organizational characteristics of 'the enterprise' can be found to some degree in other spheres of regulated activity.

3 SOCIOLOGICAL CONCERN OVER THE BUSINESS ENTERPRISE

The rise of the modern business enterprise accompanied the processes of industrialization, and the interest shown by sociologists in the enterprise was linked with their concern over the development of industrial society in general. Sociologists do not employ the concept of 'industrial society' literally to describe a society whose livelihood depends on industry as such. Since this would be true of almost any society, such a definition would give the concept little discriminatory value. Instead, the term 'industrial society' normally refers to a society which employs a distinctive type of industry to a certain degree of intensity, and which in consequence is characterized by a relatively complex occupational and social organization, by rapid technical progress, and by continuous social change (Faunce, 1968). A society of this type in its contemporary setting is what we shall call a 'modern industrial society'.[3]

The course of industrialization and the development of the business enterprise in nineteenth-century Europe and the United States gave rise to social changes which were keenly observed by some sociological pioneers. Engels (1845), for example, vividly recorded the human misery which was the lot of many sections of the English industrial working classes. The growing economic and political power of the new entrepreneurial middle class, the strident moralistic ideology which legitimated this, the contrast in wealth and the bitterness of social conflict, the increasing specialization and trivia-

---

[3] This conception of modern industrial society is subject to two provisos:

(i) No single criterion of industrialization is entirely satisfactory. Andreski referred to the distinctive type of industry in suggesting that a society can be classed as industrial if it subsists on the products of 'big

lization of manual work, and the decreasing autonomy of employees—these were among the accompaniments of early industrialization which not only manifested themselves in contemporary events but which found explanation in the new sociology, particularly that of Karl Marx.

It is from the insights of Marx that much of present-day sociological concern over the business enterprise derives. His analysis of alienation, his recognition of the interdependence between social relationships within the enterprise and those outside it, and his predictions as to the evolving pattern of business ownership still provide the starting point for present-day analysis, as will become evident in the chapters to follow. Marx, more than any other early sociologist, recognized that the business enterprise was the institution which had to take a central place in one's understanding of the processes of industrial society. For Marx, it had already become the leading social institution (Bottomore & Rubel, 1956).

At a later date and in the context of American society, Thorstein Veblen provided a further seminal analysis of the business enterprise. Writing shortly after the formation of the great American business trusts in the late 1880s and early 1890s, Veblen anxiously sought to expose the exploitation and waste of resources and human skill which he saw developing under the increasing control of business by financiers—a stage in capitalist development which Marx had predicted (Riesman, 1953). Thirdly, Max Weber argued from his classic historical sociology that Calvinism had been directly conducive to the development of the thriftful habits and rationality of conduct which were an aid to the growth and

---

and complicated machines' (1964, p. 14). Reference to the occupational concomitants of industrialization provide less ambiguous criteria such as the proportion of a society's working population which is engaged in non-agricultural production, or the proportion of national income deriving from manufacturing and associated service industries. A problem with these latter criteria is whether tertiary (service) employment is of the type associated with industrialization or not.

(ii) Applying these criteria immediately indicates that countries today range along scales of industrialization (cf. Florence, 1964, pp. 4–5; UN 1965: Tables 2, 3 & 4; EEC, 1966, Table 7). The concept of 'modern industrial society' should not therefore be used to imply that industrial societies are equally industrialized, or that there is any clear threshold of industrialization (cf. Birnbaum, 1964).

successful administration of capitalist business enterprises (Weber, 1930). At the same time, he feared that the extension of the consequent legal-rational bureaucratic mode of organization would inflict a new tyranny on those members of society who were subject to it; a power based on ordered expertise against which even elected political representatives were at a disadvantage. Weber's 'ideal-type' conceptualization of bureaucracy has provided a point of reference for many subsequent studies of organization (Gerth & Mills, 1946).

These three pioneering sociologists, Marx, Veblen and Weber, are names which will necessarily re-appear in our discussion of the business enterprise. They pre-eminently have led the way in plotting out the main issues of sociological concern relevant to the chosen theme of this book, namely the place of the business enterprise in modern industrial society. The sociological importance of this theme derives from the interdependence between business enterprise and other institutions in societies where business organizations account for most employment and dispose of very considerable resources. The interest of Marx, Veblen and Weber centred around this enormous concentration of business power and its pervasive consequences for society in general. The sociological pioneers were concerned as to who controlled such power, the means whereby such control was maintained, and whether both these means and the uses to which business power was put were socially legitimate. In, for instance, Marx's insistence that property-ownership provided the key to industrial control and determined the purposes to which that control was utilized, and in Weber's extension of this analysis indicating office-holding as an alternative source of control, can be distinguished the essence of the great debate over the relevance of industrial ownership for the maintenance of socially acceptable business policies. The major issues raised by these founding-fathers have, as we shall see, been reflected in more recent sociology, though this reflection is often dimmed by the acceptance of analytical perspectives which assume away problems such as the determination of business objectives, and by the consequent preoccupation of many researchers with technical minutiae of minor organizational mechanics.

This short book attempts to review contributions to our knowledge and understanding of the business enterprise in

modern industrial society. It selects some of the major sociological issues associated with this subject, discussing schemes
of analysis and available research which assist towards the
clarification of those issues. In places it will prove necessary
to assess a primarily sociological issue by reference to economic
and psychological research. As some writers have recognized
(e.g. Arensberg, 1942; Parsons & Smelser, 1957), the theme of
this book presents a noteworthy case where a sociological
perspective (that of collectivities and action within them)
provides an integrating framework for contributions from the
social sciences as a whole.

The coverage of a short review is necessarily limited and
selective. We have, for instance, chosen not to give an
adequate portrayal of structure and behaviour within business
enterprises since many sources on this topic are already
available to the reader. (These include March & Simon, 1958;
Dalton, 1959; Burns & Stalker, 1961; Blau & Scott, 1963;
March, 1965; Parker *et al.*, 1968, Part II). We also omit some
issues concerning the sociology of work and labour relations
which are covered by Alan Fox's contribution to this series.

Another point to note is that the nature of previous sociological enquiry and the scope of available research will cause
this book to focus primarily on the business enterprise in
capitalist industrial societies, especially the USA and the UK.
However, we shall refer where appropriate to the equivalent
organization in communist societies for purposes of comparison. In such cases, it will be important to remember that
identical values do not apply, and further that organizationally the enterprise in communist societies is normally
equivalent to the establishment or plant in western industry,
long-range planning being undertaken at a higher level by
the state bureaucracy (Richman, 1965; Nove, 1969). Moreover, the variety of types of business enterprise in capitalist
societies should be borne in mind as placing a limit on the
generality of our subsequent discussion.

The issues on which we shall concentrate emerge from a
consideration of the business enterprise as a central institution within modern industrial society. The chapters of this
book reflect firstly the analytical problem of how we should
conceptualize the business enterprise in relation to its social
environment, and secondly the sociological concern over the
consequences of interdependence between business and

society. The initial conceptualization of the business enterprise is of considerable sociological importance since the assumptions one makes at that stage either inhibit or encourage the subsequent asking of given questions about the structure and social role of business. The plan of our chapters reflects this point of view:

(i) Chapter II asks how one might conceptualize the business enterprise in its social environment, and how one can analyse the nature of interaction between the two. It also attempts to illustrate the effect of different social environments on business operations. The light which this chapter can throw on the nature of business enterprise serves as an underpinning for and a bridge towards the remainder of the book.

(ii) A major dimension of interaction between business and environment is that of power. The widespread consequences of business power have raised questions of who wields this power, to what ends, and subject to what social controls? These questions have particularly been linked to debate over the separation of business control from ownership and its likely consequences. They form the subject-matter of Chapter III.

(iii) The social concern over the control of business which is evident in modern industrial society is both encouraged by, and itself encourages, a recognition that business operations extensively influence the quality of people's lives. Marx's analysis of alienation sharpened sociological awareness of this point at an early stage. The extent and nature of the social problems which are associated with the business enterprise constitute a third major issue which is discussed in Chapter IV.

(iv) In Chapter V we note that the application of social criteria to the performance of the business enterprise raises the further issue of how far these are compatible with its fundamentally economic rationale. This issue leads on to the important question of how much choice is available in the design of business organization to permit an improvement in both its overall social and economic performance.

(v) Finally, emerging trends are relevant to an assessment of the business enterprise in the future. Chapter VI examines such trends and their social consequences, particularly the emerging patterns associated with the rapid technical progress of modern industrial societies today.

CHAPTER II

The Business Enterprise in a Social Environment

1 QUESTIONS OF ANALYTICAL PERSPECTIVE

Writers on the business enterprise show considerable differences in the amount of attention they have paid to the social environment,[1] and in their conceptions of the enterprise as a social institution. These two factors are related in so far as those whose interest lies primarily within the boundaries of the enterprise—usually an interest in improving its technical efficiency—place themselves in a less favourable position to examine its wider social role. This is illustrated by fairly recent writing associated with the so-called 'human relations' school and with certain branches of 'organization theory', which has been justly criticized for treating business enterprises almost as though they were self-contained entities operating in a socio-economic vacuum (Siegel, 1957; Cunnison, 1966).[2] A great deal of organization theory has in the past adopted an implicitly structural-functional orientation, in which the environment (when it *is* considered) is seen simply as a means to the organization's operation and survival, or at most as a limiting factor (cf. Silverman, 1968a).

[1] Henceforth simply called 'environment', and referring to those societal features with which a business enterprise is brought into direct contact through its operations and through the various social roles occupied by its members.

[2] This criticism is appropriate not so much to the human relations philosophers such as Whitehead (1936) and Mayo (1945) as to the many management theorists who derived inspiration from them. For Whitehead and Mayo were active exponents of a new social role for the business enterprise which involved a definite view as to its relationship with the environment.

The sociological tradition, on the other hand, approaches the business enterprise primarily from an interest in its environment; that is, from an interest in its relationship with other social institutions. Thus one finds that the close and necessary connections between business enterprises and their environments were recognized in the pioneering analysis of Marx (Bottomore & Rubel, 1956, Part III) and of Weber (Gerth & Mills, 1946, Chapter VIII; Lazarsfeld & Oberschall, 1965). The theoretical perspectives which sociologists have applied to the role of the enterprise in society range considerably, from the functionalist (such as Parsons & Smelser, 1957) to the Marxist (such as Aaronovitch, 1955). From such perspectives derive varying conceptions of the business enterprise itself—(i) as a functionally integrated and normally harmonious system which is directed towards the attainment of a set of goals that all its members hold in common; (ii) as a somewhat uneasy coalition of economic convenience in which the pursuit of conflicting sectional interests is balanced against the mutual benefits of co-operation; or (iii) as a potentially unstable arrangement whereby the propertyless and oppressed many are exploited for the private gain of a privileged controlling elite.

A further question of analytical perspective concerns the degree of comprehensiveness which is followed with respect to the many variables and processes involved in this field of study. Most sociologists seeking to explain particular characteristics of the business enterprise have restricted their analysis to selected environmental variables. The attitudes and behaviour of groups within enterprises have, for instance, been explained with reference to their membership of certain types of community outside the enterprise—for instance, local (Kerr & Siegel, 1954; Dennis *et al.*, 1957); occupational (Lipset *et al.*, 1956); religious (Child, 1964); or national-cum-regional communities (Abegglen, 1958; Rimlinger, 1959). Similarly, reference has been made to features in the economic environment in order to account for behaviour within enterprises (e.g. Goode & Fowler, 1949; Siegel, 1957; March & Simon, 1958; Lupton, 1963; Goldthorpe, 1966), and to define the organizational problems of enterprises as operating units (Burns & Stalker, 1961; Lawrence & Lorsch, 1967).

Although studies such as these have contributed in important ways to our understanding of the business enterprise in relation to its environment, this was usually not the level of analysis upon which their conceptual frameworks were designed to focus. We are left therefore still groping towards a comprehensive framework for analysing business environments, while adequate models[3] of interaction between types of enterprise and types of environment are not yet available. In moving towards these objectives, considerable scope would seem to exist for linking together the different perspectives and areas of interest of sociologists and economists—for instance, the study of community with that of market in so far as both are aspects of business environment. Hitherto, it has been possible to accuse each discipline of oversimplification through ignoring the contributions of the other (cf. Gordon, 1961, Preface), though recently some sociologists (Parsons & Smelser, 1957; Lupton, 1963; Cunnison, 1966) and some 'managerial' economists (Cyert & March, 1963; Marris, 1964; Williamson, 1964) have begun to narrow this conceptual gap.

2 THE NATURE OF BUSINESS ENVIRONMENT

It will assist our subsequent understanding of the business enterprise as a social institution, and our critical assessment of models which purport to describe its interaction with other areas of society, if we first attempt some classification of business environment. This classification should bring into sharper focus those sectors of society with which in different ways business enterprises are particularly closely linked.

Sociologists have only infrequently attempted to provide typologies of the business environment. Homans (1951) argued that any social system exists within a three-part environment comprising physical, cultural and technological sectors, an analysis which can be applied to the business

---

[3] Willer (1967) provides a useful discussion of the different types of model which may be utilized in sociology. He defines a model as 'a conceptualization of a group of phenomena, constructed by means of a rationale, where the ultimate purpose is to furnish the terms and relations, the propositions, of a formal system which, if validated, becomes theory' (p. 15).

enterprise. Dill conceptualized four major sectors making up the 'task environment' of two Norwegian enterprises which he studied. These sectors comprised customers, suppliers, competitors and regulating groups—task environment was thus primarily economic in nature (Dill, 1958; also cf. Dill, 1965). Lupton (1963) concluded a study of workplace behaviour with an *ex post facto* categorization of determining variables, among which he distinguished a number of external factors relating primarily to the economic environment. Cunnison (1966) in another participant observation study of shopfloor behaviour broadened Lupton's framework to include environmental features such as employees' social class, local community and residential group. Blau and Scott (1963) have provided a comprehensive review of organizational environments, including a recognition of the cross cultural differences which we discuss later in this chapter; but their contribution lacks a conceptual framework.

There is some choice as to how the main sectors of business environment are distinguished and defined.[4] Boddewyn (1967), building on the work of Parsons and Smelser (1957) and Levy (1952), has proposed a classification in terms of physical, economic, political, social and cultural environments. We shall briefly explore a similar classification of business environment that omits the physical sector (which in itself is of less sociological interest) but elaborates the economic sector, In our scheme, business environment is taken to comprise: (i) product markets; (ii) factor markets; (iii) technical knowledge; (iv) political environment; and (v) socio-cultural environment. This classification is primarily by spheres of activity and influence, and may not correspond to specific organizations with which a given business enterprise has to deal. Thus a trade union may operate both in a factor market and through political pressures; and it may also be the harbourage of certain cultural values.

(i) and (ii) A market may be defined as 'typically an institution that brings all sellers and buyers into communication with one another for the purpose of exchanging economic goods and money for current or future delivery' (Vatter,

---

[4] A choice arises because not all features in the environment of business enterprises are equally relevant in different situations for our understanding of business behaviour.

1964; p. 407). This definition is sufficiently broad to account for economic exchange under a variety of systems ranging from the state administered markets of the USSR (Nove, 1969), through the mixed 'market socialism' of Yugoslavia (Singleton & Topham, 1963) to the less centrally administered markets of western societies.[5] Vatter's definition also immediately suggests certain strategic features of a business enterprise's market environment. It raises the question of market structure in terms of the size distributions of buyers and sellers, the extent of their organization and so on. It also points to the market context as one of exchange and bargaining, and hence raises the question of behaviours and strategies. Economists have tended to concentrate their attentions on the more easily ascertainable features of market structure (e.g. Bain, 1959; Oxenfeld, 1963), though market behaviour is the more significant aspect of business environment and cannot necessarily be inferred from structural conditions (Evely & Little, 1960; Allen, 1966).

Returning to the original distinction between (i) product and (ii) factor markets, the former comprise the environment in which business organizations sell their outputs, while factor markets are the locus of transactions through which those organizations obtain necessary resources (factors of production).

(iii) Technical knowledge as a sector of the environment of business enterprise comprises the body of knowledge about (a) scientific principles and discoveries, and (b) existing and previous industrial processes, resources of power and materials, methods of transmission and communication, and methods of administration which are thought to be relevant to the production or improvement of goods and services (a definition adapted from Burns, 1964, p. 716). It is impossible to quantify precisely the amount of available technical knowledge that is pertinent to particular industries. It is, however, possible to utilize several indicators of (a) the resources which are applied to the development of new technical knowledge (such as expenditures on research and development, or the

---

[5] Exactly how administered the capitalist market system is, and the forms of its administration, are the subject of much current debate, stimulated particularly by critics of traditional economic assumptions such as Galbraith (1967). See Chapters IV and VI below.

numbers of qualified scientists and engineers in employment) and indicators of (b) the rate at which technical knowledge is developing (such as the volume and value of new patents).

(iv) The political environment of business enterprises refers to those non-business organizations and institutions, primarily agencies of the state, political parties or trade unions, whose actions may influence the rules under which enterprises can operate. In all modern industrial societies, the institution which impinges most dramatically upon the affairs of business enterprises is the state in its various organized forms and activities. The extreme case is to be found in communist societies, particularly the USSR and China, where the enterprise itself is little more than an organ of the State (cf. Richman, 1965; Nove, 1969 and other sources in the bibliography).

(v) The variables to which the concept of socio-cultural environment refers are difficult to distinguish empirically. They are intangible and indiscrete; they are also manifested in some of the factors which we have classified within the other sectors of business environment. Socio-cultural variables are those orientations and values, translated in this case into attitudes towards the business enterprise, which can be ascribed in their origin to ethnic, religious, regional, class and other social memberships. Many of these social memberships may be identified through the type of family to which people belong, while a concept such as 'life style' allows us to describe some of the visible consequences of socio-cultural values (cf. Burns, 1966a). At a more general level, social memberships can be subsumed by the concept of 'community', particularly if one does not insist that this must be linked to the notion of a specified territorial base (cf. Sjoberg, 1964). The 'communities' which identify the socio-cultural sector of business environment can then be defined in terms of several criteria which may or may not overlap, such as geographical, occupational, ethnic, political or religious.

An interesting example of how socio-cultural factors can relate to behaviour within the enterprise has been provided by Millward (1968). He found that young unmarried girls employed as operatives in Lancashire companies responded differently to financial incentive schemes according to whether or not they were 'on board' at home—that is, whether they gave their pay-packets to their mothers and received pocket-money in return or instead kept their pay-packet and paid their mothers for board and lodging only. 'The importance of the institution of "board",' Millward concludes, 'is that it highlights a point at which the family status of the young girl changes and brings about changes in her behaviour at work' (p. 162).

Emery and Trist (1965) have argued in an important paper that we should give attention to the processes through which sectors of organizational environment become related to each other. They employ the concept of the 'causal texture of the environment' to account for those interrelationships which are confined to the environment itself. This causal texture can be regarded as a quasi-independent domain since the extent of any particular environment can only be conceptualized with reference to a focal organization—in our case a focal business enterprise. Emery and Trist postulate four ideal types of organizational environment, ranging from a 'placid, randomised' type to a 'turbulent field' type, the differentiation between types being expressed in terms of the degree to which systems within the environment are interdependent. Thus 'turbulence' is characterized by complex and rapidly changing causal interconnectedness within the environment.

The four types of organizational environment presented by Emery and Trist are so over-simplified at present as to be of doubtful utility,[6] but their underlying concept of causal texture is of considerable importance. It is readily supported even by the inadequate knowledge currently available on environmental processes. Thus the interrelationship between product and factor market conditions is a commonplace of economic analysis—in essence, the demand for resources depends on the conditions under which products can be disposed, while these conditions may themselves be affected by the income levels of resource providers (Lipsey, 1966). The influence which product market structure may exert over the rate of growth in technical knowledge has been the subject of much debate and several important studies (Galbraith, 1952; Jewkes *et al.*, 1958; Mansfield, 1963a & 1964a; Hamberg,

---

[6] Terreberry (1968) has attempted, with no remarkable result, to elaborate and extend the Emery-Trist analysis.

1964). Governments and their agencies exercise a multifarious influence on the advance of technical knowledge through general educational policies and specific research contracts (Grossfield, 1967). They exercise a similar degree of influence on market conditions through general economic regulation and through specific measures such as antimonopoly legislation in capitalist societies (Neale, 1966; Allen, 1968), and measures to control supplies and distribution in communist societies (Nove, 1969).

Two major conclusions to be drawn from the analysis so far are (i) that the environment of the business enterprise comprises several sectors, and (ii) that these sectors are interrelated independently of any one business organization.[7] Thus any comprehensive model of interaction between business enterprise and environment must contain multiple components and processes. It should allow for the possibility that actions deriving from an enterprise *vis à vis* a given sector of its environment may stimulate a series of environmental processes which in their turn lead to action deriving from another environmental sector *vis à vis* the enterprise. This complex 'feed-back' pattern can equally operate the other way around, since the business enterprise itself encompasses a number of different yet interacting components, such as membership groups, administrative structure, and technology.[8]

3 COMPARATIVE BUSINESS ENVIRONMENTS

Classification of the sectors of business environment assists a more precise comparison between the different configurations which may be found among modern industrial societies. As we note in Chapter VI, an impetus towards making such comparison has come from the feeling that the process of industrialization sets up pressures towards similar business structures and relationships with at least the economic and technical environments, regardless of the diverse political systems and socio-cultural values which prevail in different

---

[7] This is, of course, not to state that they are *only* interrelated independently of a focal business enterprise.

[8] Part II of Parker *et al.* (1968) is concerned with the internal structure of industrial organizations and reviews a wide selection of relevant research.

societies. This interest in the possibility of similar patterns of development among industrial countries, a possibility which encourages those who hope for a reconciliation between rival economic and social systems, may sometimes detract from a full consideration of research which points in the other direction—towards extensive cross-cultural differences in business environment. In this section we take a brief look at this research, in order to illustrate some of the previous analysis and to provide a groundwork for later discussion.

Nath (1968) has compiled a valuable review of 'cross-cultural management research'. He indicates that since the Second World War there has been a marked quickening of interest among social scientists in the influence exerted by societal norms and cultural values over business operations. The practical importance of this question has been highlighted by the experience of internationally based companies which are discovering that a manager who is successful in one country does not necessarily operate so well in another. Nath classifies cross-cultural research into ten types ranging from purely documentary studies to field experiments.

Although it is of varying reliability, there is a considerable weight of evidence to indicate that inter-societal differences do affect business enterprises over and above the common economic and technical exigencies which such enterprises may share. For instance, Rimlinger (1959) compared the strike propensities of coalminers in the USA, UK, Western Germany and France, finding that the first two countries had substantially more strikes and strike losses. He therefore argued that the high strike propensity associated with the industrial environment of mining (cf. Kerr & Siegel, 1954) may be reinforced or weakened according to the particular socio-cultural environment. Other investigations into international patterns of strike activity have also suggested that features specific to business environments in particular societies are important. Among such features are the organization and unity of labour movements, the strength of labour representation in the political field, and the extent and development of institutional arrangements in industrial relations (Ross & Irwin, 1951; Ross & Hartman, 1960).

Abegglen (1958) compared the social organization of

Japanese and United States factories. He found that the organizational norms of Japanese factories were less sharply differentiated from those of other social institutions such as the family, and that these norms indicated a less pronounced break in Japanese industry with the values of a fairly recent feudal past. Japanese organizational norms included relatively personalized and collectivity-oriented relationships, rigid stratification, and an assumption that employees joined their companies for life. Abegglen in effect was able to account for the peculiar organizational features of Japanese factories by reference to the influence of prevailing cultural values. Likewise Crozier (1964), in a study which combines inspired analysis with somewhat haphazardly collected empirical data, has attempted to compare norms prevailing in French, Russian, American and British societies as independent variables which give rise to typically different organizational structures. Armstrong (1965) has also concluded that the marked differences between Russian and West European administrative behaviour do not result solely from varying levels and rates of industrialization and that they indicate in addition the effect of fundamentally differing political ideologies.

A range of studies have pointed to international differences in management styles or philosophies (Nath 1968 refers to many of these studies; in addition see Nowotny 1964 and Haire *et al.*, 1966). Similarly, a number of studies have pointed to the different expectations held of the work situation by employees of different nationalities. Richardson (1956) compared British and American merchant ship crews and found differences in their attitudes towards an acceptance of authority. French, Israel and Ås (1960) replicated the classic American study by Coch and French (1948) in Norway, and found differences in employees' reactions to opportunities of participation in organizational decision-making. These differences appeared to derive in part from the different employee expectations in the two countries as to what were legitimate participative procedures. Cortis (1962) and Whitehill (1964) respectively found noticeable differences in the attitudes of Bantu compared with European workers, and in those of Japanese compared with American blue-collar employees.

So while it *is* possible to point out certain organizational similarities among business enterprises located in different industrial societies, and to relate these similarities to comparable economic or technical necessities and opportunities, it is evident that socio-cultural and political differences play an important and independent determining role as well. Research which suggests cross-cultural similarities (such as the finding by Likert 1963 that similar supervisory styles are the most productive in the USA, India, England and Japan), is often countered by other evidence suggesting cross-cultural differentiation (as with the study by Whyte and Williams 1963 which compared supervisory style and employee satisfaction with supervision in the United States and Peru). The examination by Udy (1959) of data from 150 non-industrial societies is relevant in this context since his conclusions point both to certain common inter-societal requirements for industrialization and to the critical independent role of cultural supports. His evidence led him to the view that the most important factor in promoting industrialization is not so much the introduction of the complex bureaucratic organizational forms found in industrialized societies as the establishment of institutional supports for the required social orientations of achievement, specificity and universalism (cf. Parsons, 1952).

There is an urgent need to place research on comparative business environments into a more systematic conceptual framework, and on to a sounder methodological basis, before sociologists can be more precise in assessing the influence of those environments on the business enterprise. Existing research, particularly relating to work attitudes and patterns of industrial conflict, already suggests the presence of several broad groupings among modern industrial societies distinguishable with respect to features of business environment—groupings such as North America, Northern Europe, Mediterranean, Eastern Europe (possibly treating Yugoslavia as a special case), and Japan. The presence of such groupings requires further confirmation and elaboration.

4 INTERACTION OF BUSINESS ENTERPRISE AND ENVIRONMENT—CONCEPTS AND MODELS

We have so far considered a scheme for classifying those aspects of society which impinge sufficiently closely upon a business enterprise as to be called its environment. We have also illustrated how environmental features can differ substantially between societies. Our discussion has already referred to some of the ways in which environmental variables relate to behaviour within, and the structure of, business enterprises. There are available to the reader several sources which have systematically collected together research on the interaction between business enterprises and other sectors of modern industrial societies; sectors such as local communities, and educational, family, political or stratification systems (Schneider, 1957, Part 4; Miller & Form, 1964, Chapters 4 & 18; Parker *et al.*, 1968, Part I). Other writers have explored the interaction between large business enterprises and their international environments (e.g. Vernon, 1959; Kronstein, 1965). Subsequent chapters of this book will themselves illustrate certain areas of interaction between the business enterprise and its environment—in connection with socio-political controls over business (Chapter III), with the influence of the enterprise over the quality of life open to members of society (Chapter IV), and with the extent of economic and technical constraints on the structure and policies of enterprises both now (Chapter V) and in the emerging future (Chapter VI). Rather than presenting more descriptive material, the remainder of this chapter is addressed to the problem of how the sociologist may conceptualize the relationships which available research indicates may exist between a business enterprise and its environment.

An analysis of interaction between the business enterprise and its environment entails (i) some consideration of the boundary between the two, and (ii) the development of conceptual schemes and models appropriate for the interactive processes to be studied. The assessment of available schemes of analysis (in Section iii) will help to clarify a point we made earlier, namely that, how one regards the business enterprise is closely associated with one's conception of its predominant relationships to the social environment.

(i) The general concept of a boundary is inherent in any consideration of relationships between two or more components, while the particular concept of organizational boundary is implicit in any distinction between a business enterprise and its environment. However, the way in which organizational boundary should be described, and whether it need be distinguished at all, has been a matter of uncertainty.

It is possible to discuss business organizations without specifying their boundaries as do March and Simon (1958), but this omission tends (a) to encourage a purely intra-organizational, 'closed-system' analysis, and (b) to undermine the conceptual clarity which is essential if analysis in this area is to advance further than mere non-comparative description. It has, at the same time, to be admitted that the empirical determination of organizational boundary presents considerable difficulties. Certainly, any attempt to conceive of organizational boundary as a simple, sharp and single line is misleading. It may be more realistically viewed as a composite 'semi-permeable membrane' (Goffman, 1957). There are varying degrees of mutual permeation between business organizations and their environments along several fronts and at several organizational levels. The clarity with which one can distinguish empirically the boundary of a business enterprise will differ as between the various components entering into interchange with the environment. For instance, materials and products enter and leave an enterprise at discrete, recognizable points both physically and in terms of ownership. In contrast, the multiple roles and overlapping commitments held by the various employees of a business enterprise renders the empirical distinction of an enterprise boundary extremely tenuous in their case (Schein, 1965, p. 89).

(ii) In recent decades the business environment has become increasingly characterized by large and organized units with the development of consumer organizations, the extended activities of governmental bureaucracies, the extension (at least until recently) of trade union representation, and the growing scale of other enterprises themselves (cf. Warner *et al.*, 1967). Partly for this reason the employment of inter-organizational analysis has enjoyed growing popularity among sociologists as a method for studying interaction between business enterprises and their environments. This mode of analysis has contributed many of the classificatory schemes and the concepts which are available today. However, these still exhibit considerable diversity and lack an adequate theoretical base. Indeed, the theoretical assumption which is implied in many inter-organizational concepts, namely that an organization can be treated as a unity, is not wholly satisfactory from a sociological point of view. Among available inter-organizational analyses, the work of Evan, Guetzkow, Thompson and McEwen, Aiken and Hage is particularly noteworthy.

Evan (1965) has proposed the concept of the 'organization-set', which is analogous to Merton's 'role-set' for individuals (Merton, 1957). Relations between a focal organization and the members of its organization-set are in fact seen as being mediated by the role-sets of boundary personnel, such as buyers or salesmen in the case of a business enterprise. Evan thus offers a conceptual tool for distinguishing the environmental organizations or groups with which a focal business organization interacts. Guetzkow (1966) has attempted to classify the interactions within an organization-set both by location and by intrinsic features. Thompson and McEwen (1958) had suggested earlier a four-fold classification of relationships between an organization and environmental agencies in respect of setting goals. These relationships, they argued, may represent four strategies: (a) competition, or one of three forms of co-operation—(b) bargaining, (c) co-optation and (d) coalition.

Thompson and McEwen's analysis serves to highlight the important dimension of power in relations between the business enterprise and other social institutions, a dimension to which we return later (in Chapter III) with special emphasis on the goals and responsibilities of business leaders. Their actual classification is useful in that it indicates how the interaction of a business enterprise with its environment may take the form not only of exchange (as in bargaining) but of joint developments as well. Aiken and Hage (1967) have considered relationships between organizations where these have taken the form of joint programmes, such as combined research programmes undertaken by different firms or combined services offered by welfare agencies. Aiken and Hage point out that this area of investigation has been neglected by comparison with the amount of analysis which has adopted exchange as the focal characteristic of inter-organizational relationships (cf. the study by Levine & White, 1961; and discussions by Parsons & Smelser, 1957; Litwak & Hylton, 1962; Barth, 1963; Rice, 1963).

Finally, reference must be made to the work of Form & Miller (1960) who have presented a valuable analysis of relationships between industry and community which is not confined to an inter-organizational perspective. They, too, highlight the dimension of power, distinguishing five types of relationship in terms of the relative power of employers, labour unions and community institutions to determine working conditions and other business decisions.

The above examples indicate that there are a number of classificatory and conceptual schemes available for the analysis of business enterprise and its environment. But when we look for more advanced stages of theory construction in this area, the contributions of sociologists and organization theorists are few and disappointing. There are really only two attempts to construct models of interaction between business and environment which are noteworthy.[9] The first model is that proposed by Parsons and Smelser (Parsons, 1956; Parsons & Smelser, 1957), the second has been put forward by Rice (1963). Both are functionalist in that they analyse interaction in terms of its contribution towards institutional maintenance and survival, and both suffer the usual functionalist limitations regarding the role of power and conflict. The Parsons/Smelser model takes society as its unit of analysis and is concerned with many interaction processes, while Rice takes the business enterprise as his unit of analysis and considers interaction with the economic environment only.

Parsons and Smelser present what may be called a *'system-subsystem model'* in that business enterprises (indeed, the whole economy) are seen as providing a primarily adaptive function for society, with their goals being established exclusively by the environment in terms of the functional requirements of society as a whole. The rationale and continued integration of a business enterprise is assumed to centre on commonly accepted goals which are oriented to the fulfilment of general social needs. Although we shall see that their functionalist model is open to criticism, Parsons and Smelser's

[9] The economic theory of oligopoly (cf. Fellner, 1949) offers a sophisticated approach to certain areas of interaction between the business enterprise and its environment, which may become profitably wedded to the work of organization theorists. Cyert and March (1963) represent a move in this direction.

analysis possesses two considerable merits. First, because society is their unit of analysis they identify a wide range of environmental components. They recognize the relatedness of these components, and while they treat all sections of the environment as collectivities they also allow at least implicitly that their degrees of organization may vary considerably—as between, say, 'families' and 'government'. Second, Parsons and Smelser employ the concept of 'boundary interchange' to indicate the functional interaction between the economic and other social systems. This usefully draws attention to the notions of boundary and exchange mentioned previously.

Rice, in his model, also adopts a socially harmonious view of the business enterprise, a leading assumption being that a 'primary task' such as profit-making can be posited for the whole enterprise. The Rice model then concentrates on those economic transactions with the environment upon which profitable operations depend. In essence, this is a *'system-feedback model'*, in which the business enterprise is depicted as attempting to maintain a 'steady state' by means of an input $\rightarrow$ conversion $\rightarrow$ output process, with money obtained from the product market being 'fed back' to factor markets in order to secure new inputs. A steady state is maintained so long as the enterprise performs adequately in its economic environment. Although our summary has not done it full justice, the Rice model is very elementary viewed from the point of economic theory; but it has the merit of indicating the fundamentally economic rationale of the business enterprise. Schein has suggested (1965, pp. 90–1) that a combination of Rice's model with Trist's concept of the enterprise as a socio-technical system[10] greatly extends the former and draws attention to the presence of multiple channels of interaction between an enterprise and its environment. This interaction can then be seen as representing various constraints upon the operation of a business enterprise—market (especially consumer preferences), technical (available know-how), and social (employee expectations, norms and values).

(iii) Both the Parsons/Smelser and Rice models of business enterprises and their environments are 'open system' models. They are system models in that they depend on a conception of the business enterprise as an integrated unit comprising

[10] This concept is considered in Chapter V.

working parts which normally interrelate in such a way as to maintain that unit's survival. They are *open* system models in that they take account of interaction between given units of analysis and their environments: between an enterprise and its environment, between a department of an enterprise and the whole organization, and so on. Open system analysis has gained considerable favour among students of business and other organizations, Katz and Kahn (1966) and Miller and Rice (1967) being cases in point. Apart from its stress on environment, open system analysis offers other advantages. For instance, its emphasis on multiple interaction between parts draws attention to the effects of a change in one part of the system on the other parts, while the notion of 'system' itself reminds one that organizations are collectivities and are more than the sum of their parts.

However, open system analysis has often in practice been employed in a manner which distorts sociological realities. The idea of a business enterprise as a system suggests the presence of a consciously designed set of arrangements to maintain the enterprise's survival and prosperity. This implication is acceptable so long as one remembers that this design reflects the purposes of the designers. What cannot be accepted without further critical enquiry is the supposition that the policies and structure of a business enterprise are fully acceptable to its other member groups, or that such groups will agree to work to the design which is set down for them. Most system models of the business enterprise developed so far have ignored or minimized this qualification. They have instead tended to impute to the enterprise a unified set of goals which are somehow established and maintained over and above the objectives of its members. This tendency towards a reification of the business enterprise is reinforced in some writings by their reliance on an analogy with the organic biological system which has, of course, an existence in its own right. The use of an organic analogy also implies that the normal 'healthy' condition of an enterprise consists in a harmonious and lasting integration of its parts. That different groups which are party to an enterprise may employ different referents for assessing its 'health' is generally not considered by system theorists. Such quasi-metaphysical manœuvres do little more than disguise an uncritical acceptance of objectives set down by system controllers (i.e. managers) and the search for mechanisms whereby such objectives, rather than others, may be attained. This restricted orientation towards the business enterprise as a field of study has been strongly rejected by many sociologists (e.g. Banks, 1963a; Brown, 1967; Albrow, 1968; Silverman, 1968a, 1968b).

The development of open system analysis was stimulated by a realization that most human relations theory had failed to take sufficient account of the business environment. However, while system analyses have referred to the business environment, their assumptions about that environment are still in many instances over-simplified. Such over-simplifications directly contribute to the deficiencies in the system theorists' conceptualizations of the business enterprise itself. Thus Parsons is able to regard the enterprise as a functionally integrated social unit because he assumes that its goals are determined in accord with agreed societal values. He does not adequately allow either for the existence of differing social expectations regarding the legitimate role of business, or for the possibility that business leaders may be powerful enough to ignore socially valued objectives if it is in their interest to do so (a problem discussed in Chapter III). Rice, too, can only support his concept of an enterprise's 'primary task' by confining his analysis of interaction with the environment to those economic transactions which relate directly to the achievement of that postulated objective.

A serious problem with many system models is that they draw attention away from a number of sociologically interesting features which comprise an important aspect of the business enterprise and of its role in the social environment. Such features are not amenable to an organic analogy or to a functionalist approach which both stress co-operation and integration within a 'working organization' directed at a common task. For these features centre on the competing demands for income, power, prestige, status and other rewards which are placed upon an enterprise by its participants. As Burns (1966b) has pointed out, as well as being a working organization, the business enterprise also contains a 'status hierarchy' of powers and privileges, and a 'political system' in which individuals and groups seek to secure current rewards and future opportunities in fulfilment of their expectations. These expectations are derived with reference to the social roles which people occupy in the environment—as family bread-winners, as members of professional bodies, as financial speculators, or whatever the case may be. Thus allowance has to be made for the purposes which its members see a business enterprise as performing for them, and for the actions which they may take towards ensuring that those purposes are fulfilled. For this reason, many sociologists prefer to regard the business enterprise as primarily an economic association or coalition rather than simply as a productive system or organism of which the members are treated as parts without any autonomy or independent rationale of their own.[11]

Considerations such as these are raised by sociologists who subscribe to a growing school of thought which argues that the reification of institutions, organizations and structures can best be avoided by utilizing what they call a 'social action' perspective (Willener, 1964; Goldthorpe, 1966; Goldthorpe *et al.*, 1968; Silverman, 1968a). This perspective, which lies within a central Weberian tradition in sociology, is concerned in the context of the business enterprise to identify four main sets of phenomena:

(a) The goals held by, and the opportunities available to, different groups or individuals within the enterprise.

(b) The ways in which environmental factors, such as domestic circumstances, alternative employments, or community values, shape the orientations that members of the enterprise possess with respect to work, and hence the work goals they hold.

(c) The ways in which employee orientations and work goals may also be influenced by other members of the enterprise.

(d) The behaviour of groups and individuals within the

[11] Marxist sociologists would reject the organic analogy without any hesitation in so far as it was being applied to privately-owned business enterprises. On the other hand, they would probably qualify the view that enterprises were economic associations (which does imply some freedom to join and leave) by stressing that there is often an obligation on employees to join enterprises in order to secure any livelihood at all, and by arguing that this element of coercion permits those owning the enterprises to exploit employees for excessive private gain.

enterprise which can be predicted as a product of interaction between work goals and features of the enterprise which may or may not facilitate their satisfaction such as management styles, task structures or remunerations offered.

The social action approach expressed in these terms provides a framework for the analysis of group or individual decision-making throughout the business enterprise and in relation to conditions pertaining beyond its boundary. Therefore, in contrast to the organic model, social action analysis allows generally for the pluralist composition of enterprises as social organizations (cf. Fox, 1966), and particularly for the fact that the co-operation of these various parties in pursuit of an enterprise's official goals or 'primary task' is conditional upon this arrangement satisfying their purposes better than any available alternative. In other words, the permanent unity of constituent parts which is implied in an organic analogy can by no means be taken for granted. Unlike some other frames of reference, social action theory also has the advantage of not positing *a priori* either a conflictual or a co-operative model of the business enterprise, but of allowing instead for a variety of empirical possibilities.

However, it may still be necessary for some purposes to make simplifying assumptions about the action basis of behavioural and structural patterns, particularly for undertaking comparative analyses at the level of whole business organizations and their environments. For instance, it may be useful to take the predominating set of goals within an enterprise as strategic and as given in the short-term at least.[12] Similarly, although features such as organizational structure and technology are the products of many previous and continuing decision processes, it is often more practicable to regard them as relatively static, again in the short run. In other words, while accepting that the constituent features of a business enterprise, its environment and interaction between the two, are all the changing products of continuing human decision and action, it is convenient for some purposes to simplify the picture by regarding them as structured patterns. This need not mean that one seriously reifies the structural construct or imputes any functional necessity to it.

[12] See Perrow (1961) for a useful distinction of various sets of goals which may co-exist within an organization.

We are arguing, then, that it is legitimate to make simplifying assumptions when analysing the highly complex interactions between a business enterprise and its environment, so long as those assumptions are made explicit and the limits thereby imposed on one's analysis are clearly recognized. Therefore when one wishes to make simplifying assumptions about social action considerations, the implications of this simplification for one's analysis have to be borne in mind. One can see now how attempts to apply the open system models of natural science (cf. von Bertalanffy, 1950) have involved important sociological simplifications which have not usually been spelt out clearly, or even recognized at all, by the writers concerned. The result is that their work has, on balance, possibly given rise to as much confusion as enlightenment. At the same time, there are equally confusing cases when the mystical label of 'system analysis' is applied loosely and quite unnecessarily to schemes of analysis which in reality posit no more than the presence of multiple interactions between variables. If such sources of confusion were in future to be avoided, the sociological analysis of the business enterprise and its environment would benefit considerably.

5 DISCUSSION

The present chapter has gone some way towards outlining the basic framework for a comprehensive and multivariate scheme of analysis of the business enterprise and its environment. It has suggested that one is here dealing with three linked sets of relationships:

A. The business enterprise, which as Schein has put it, 'consists of many subsystems which are in dynamic interaction with one another' (1965, p. 95). Among the components of the business enterprise which contribute to these 'subsystems' are membership groups (and their objectives), administrative structure, and technology.

B. The business environment, which we divided into five main sectors. These sectors are themselves interrelated independently of any one business organization, and for this reason the environment can be described meaningfully as a 'causal texture', following Emery and Trist (1965).

C. A set of multiple interactions between the constituent

components of the enterprise (A) and the environment (B). These interactions may in a sense be 'mediated' by those attributes of an enterprise which identify it in respect of its environment. Thus its size identifies its significance within particular markets, while its location identifies its socio-cultural environment.

In its barest outline, this framework of analysis may be portrayed in the following manner, where each line represents a set of relationships:

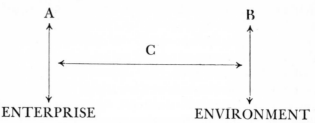

ENTERPRISE   ENVIRONMENT

An analytical perspective of this kind makes it clear that any study which is confined to selected variables within this field involves assumptions about the possible influence exerted by the excluded variables, and that such assumptions should be recognized. In addition, it usefully suggests certain lines of research which could form growth points of future sociological interest.

For example, the scheme presented above raises the question of whether there may be distinct and recurring configurations of A (variables comprising the enterprise) and of B (variables comprising the environment). Is it further the case that certain structural patterns within business enterprises are commonly, even necessarily, associated with certain environmental configurations? The answer to this question has important implications for the problems of organizational design which are discussed in Chapter V. A particular aspect of the same issue concerns the role of socio-cultural as against economic and technical factors in determining the different forms of business enterprise to be found across modern industrial societies.

The type of analysis presented in this chapter draws attention also to the question of boundaries between enterprise and environment. Here we need to establish more clearly the nature of such boundaries, indeed the sense in which one *can* distinguish organizational boundaries at the multiple points of interaction with the environment. What part is played by the occupants of boundary roles in business enterprises, by people such as salesmen, research scientists, or personnel officers, in shaping the relationship of these enterprises to those sectors of the environment with which they deal? We need to know far more, in fact, not only about the influence which may be exerted by the occupants of boundary roles, but also about the processes by which enterprises and environmental groups as a whole attempt to exert influence over each other.

In general, this whole area of sociological investigation is ready for a more comparative and multivariate approach than has hitherto been normal. It is opportune that descriptive work, of which Davis and Blomstrom (1966) provide a recent example, should give way to a more systematic assessment of how characteristics of business enterprise differ within various contexts carefully chosen for comparative purposes.[13] Due regard should also be paid to the range of causal influences involved. One of the most difficult problems facing sociologists in this respect is how to secure adequate data on environmental variables in order to establish an accurate basis for comparison between enterprises. For this reason, sociologists interested in this field will be encouraged to work more closely with economists, political scientists, and specialist students of other social institutions whose expertise is directed at important features of the business environment.

[13] Pugh *et al.* (1969) represents a pioneering step in this direction.

CHAPTER III

Private and Social Definitions of Business

1 THE PROBLEM OF BUSINESS POWER

Marx and Engels were among the first to point out tendencies towards the centralization of economic power within capitalist societies (1848, Part I). More recently, Berle and Means in their classic study of *The Modern Corporation and Private Property* (1932) argued that, in the United States at least, economic power was becoming concentrated in the hands of the large corporation. In addition, they held that the control of these large enterprises was passing from their owners into the hands of their managerial office-holders, and that this transformation was likely to have significant consequences for the criteria governing the use of business power.

The trend of industrial concentration[1] in the United States has in fact not unequivocally supported the Berle and Means prediction. There appears to have been no overall increase in concentration between the First World War and the late 1940s, although there may have been some increase more recently (Kaysen, 1959; Lintner, 1959; Shepherd, 1964; Stacey, 1966). In Britain, available evidence suggests some growth in concentration to the mid 1930s, little change to the early 1950s, and growing concentration since then (Allen, 1966; Shepherd, 1966; George, 1967). From the 1950s, tendencies towards greater concentration have been boosted by the powerful movement towards amalgamations and take-overs (Stacey, 1966).

Industrial concentration is at best an imperfect guide to business power in modern industrial society. On the one

[1] The proportion of an industry's activity, assets or employment accounted for by a few relatively large enterprises.

hand, high concentration may coexist with considerable competition between giant enterprises, or along with strenuous countervailing powers exercised by other economic or political institutions (Galbraith, 1952; Kaysen, 1959). On the other hand, it is possible to have a continued rise in the scale of particular enterprises without registering a rise in industrial concentration. And it is large size itself, as much as anything else, which has been associated with various social and political problems of business, and which has accordingly deeply concerned sociologists and other commentators.

American writers have been particularly interested in the emergence of the large business enterprise and in the concentration of powers which it represents.[2] Not only is there a larger number of such enterprises in the United States, but large corporations appear to threaten the prevailing American ideology of political pluralism. These writers have described the considerable scope of big business power today. This power operates most directly in economic terms, via decisions on investment, pricing, location, research, and product design, but it also has considerable social and political consequences in terms of employment opportunities, the operation of local community affairs, and the quality of people's lives generally (cf. especially Friedmann, 1957; Kaysen, 1959; Dill, 1965; Hacker, 1965a). As Hacker has commented, a remarkable feature of business power is how unrestrained it is in its exercise (1965a, p. 10).

Discussion about the power of large business enterprise has focused on several issues. There has been some anxiety over the influence which business leaders can exert over social welfare, particularly as there is no reason to suppose that they possess any particular aptitude or mandate for deciding on this matter (e.g. Kaysen, 1959). Considerable attention has also been given to ways by which business leaders might be held more accountable for their actions and whereby those actions themselves may be regulated (e.g. Friedmann, 1957; Rostow, 1959). However, the centre of debate over business

---

[2] This American literature has now reached enormous proportions—cf. Means, 1931; Berle & Means, 1932; Drucker, 1946; Galbraith, 1952; Boulding, 1953; Bower, 1953; Berle, 1954; Childs & Cater, 1954; Berle, 1957, 1959a; Moore, 1962; Smith, 1963; Cheit, 1964; Baran & Sweezy, 1966; Petit, 1967; and the essays in Mason, 1959; The Annals, 1962; Hacker, 1965b.

power in capitalist societies has concerned Berle and Means' thesis about the transition in large business enterprise from control by ownership to control by salaried managers who, they argued, have little or no shareholding commitment. Thus anxiety about the effects of business power has become allied with uncertainty over the legitimacy of senior management's access to that power. If it can no longer be assumed that managers are effectively accountable to the legal owners of a private business, then to whom are they, and should they be responsible? On what criteria are they, and should they be selected for office? What are their objectives, and what should they be? In general, does a 'mangerial revolution' presage a new socially responsible definition of business power? (cf. Mason, 1959, especially Introduction).

In these ways, the so-called 'divorce of ownership from control' is intimately bound up with the problem of business power. Indeed, although this notion is usually applied to privately-owned enterprise it is also relevant to a consideration of the relations between the managements and ownership representatives of publicly-owned enterprise. Berle (1959b) has made the interesting point that management power tends to operate on the margins of the law not only in the USA but in the USSR as well. With this in mind, the debate over managerial accountability and responsibility in relation to the exercise of business power can be seen to form part of the historic sociological concern over the emergence of bureaucracies as structured centres of power in modern industrial societies (cf. Michels, 1915; Gerth & Mills, 1946; Bendix, 1945; Merton *et al.*, 1952).

2 DIVORCE OF OWNERSHIP FROM CONTROL—THE CONCEPT

The concept of a 'divorce of ownership from control' expresses a postulated consequence of continuing economic changes in capitalist societies. As business enterprises grow, it is argued, they become organizationally and technologically more complex and therefore rely increasingly on the employment of specialist managers. They also issue more share capital as they expand, and this is taken up by a body of shareholders which is rapidly growing both because economic development enables more people to invest in shares and because progressive taxation tends to break up formerly large share-holdings. As share-ownership becomes more dispersed it divides control and this encourages absenteeism from company activities. The consequent power vacuum is filled by an increasingly entrenched management.

This approximates to the exposition set out by Berle and Means (1932). Although their work is generally regarded as a classic, they were not the first to recognize the trend. Marx noted a separation of management functions from ownership in mid-nineteenth-century British joint stock companies (Bottomore & Rubel, 1956, p. 153). Veblen described as a major feature of modern capitalism a conflict of interests between waste-making, oligopolistic business 'financiers' (represented by the American tycoon) and the managerial 'engineers' who were responsible for, and desirous of, increasing production. Though he held hopes for the eventual triumph of the manager-engineers, he considered that the interests of business ownership were still in the ascendancy at the time of his writing. Indeed, towards the end of his life he became increasingly pessimistic about the prospect of the manager-engineers securing a position from which they could pursue production and workmanship in the interests of the whole community (Veblen, 1904, 1914; especially Chapter V, 1921, 1923; especially Chapter VIII). Among British writers, it is interesting to note that Tawney's social critique was based on a remarkably similar, though somewhat more optimistic, analysis (1921, 1961, pp. 169–73). Alfred Marshall, the economist, briefly discussed the divorce between capital ownership and control at an equally early date (1919, Part II, Chapter VIII). At the same time many management theorists recognized, and indeed built upon, a growing role differentiation between business ownership and executive management (e.g. Lee, 1921; Sheldon, 1923; and see Child, 1969).

The concept of a divorce of ownership from control has contained certain ambiguities which have contributed to confusion and disagreements among sociologists. The notion of 'control' has typically been left undefined, yet it could imply a variety of possibilities (cf. Lockwood, 1964 on the related concept of 'power'). Does control mean the actual determination of behaviour, the ability to determine it if necessary, or the ability merely to oppose actions proposed by others? Nor is it sufficient to rely, as did Berle and Means, solely upon formal rights expressed in property-ownership or tenure of official positions for a measure of the extent to which any individual or group is actually exercising control over a business enterprise. There is also some doubt as to what the notion of 'divorce' or 'separation' should imply in respect of business ownership and control. Does it mean simply a functional differentiation between two business roles—a manifestation of growing specialization, or does it denote a fundamental opposition of financial, normative and social interests—a manifestation of an evolving system of social stratification with managers emerging as a 'new class'? There has, finally, been some confusion because of a failure to distinguish precisely the various groups which may comprise 'ownership' and 'management'. Instead, the two terms have frequently been employed in an over-simplified way to suggest monolithic social entities.

These definitional problems can be detected both in the interpretations which have been given to the idea of a divorce of ownership from control, and in the few attempts which have been made to assess the extent of the trend and the nature of its consequences.

3 DIVORCE OF OWNERSHIP FROM CONTROL—INTERPRETATION

Dahrendorf (1959, pp. 41–8) has distinguished two main interpretations of the divorce between ownership and control. He labels these the 'conservative school' which claims that ownership and control have not become separated in modern capitalist industry to any sociologically important degree, and the 'radical school' which takes the view that modern large joint-stock companies involve a complete break with previous capitalist organization.

Nichols (1967) has argued that Dahrendorf's radical school could less confusingly be termed *'managerialist'*, following Mason (1958). The adherents of this school 'not only share the belief that a separation of ownership and control has occurred but, put simply, . . . they believe that it matters, and that it has resulted in changes in business behaviour, and, by extension in business ideology' (Nichols, 1967, p. 66). Nichols distinguishes a division within the managerialist school between (i) those who argue that the new managerial controllers will be primarily self-interested—*'sectional managerialism'*; and (ii) those who argue that the actions of managers in large enterprises today accord with conceptions of social responsibility and of service to the community as a whole—*'non-sectional managerialism'*. Dahrendorf's 'conservative school' would then preferably be named the *'Marxist school'*, although some of its adherents such as C. Wright Mills have not been Marxists (Nichols, 1967, pp. 46–7).[3]

The Marxist school makes several main points in support of its conclusion that any differences between ownership and management in modern capitalism merely amount to a functional differentiation which has no real effect on the underlying structure of class relationships in society. It argues that:

(i) Because of devices such as non-voting shares and because of the difficulties of combination facing a large mass of small shareholders, large shareholders represent a concentration of ownership that is still sufficient to ensure control in the sense of preventing managers from adopting policies detrimental to their interests. In any case, ownership is now becoming more concentrated with the increasing value of holdings by institutions such as insurance companies and pension funds.

(ii) The power of large shareholders is reinforced by a system of interlocking directorships which extends their influence to other organizations, particularly financial ones, upon which the managers of a business enterprise may rely. Studies such as those by Lupton and Wilson (1959) and Aaronovitch (1961) have indicated the extent of such interlocking directorships, as well as kinship links, in Britain. Moreover, financial institutions may both represent large

---

[3] Even more misleading than his use of labels with strong political connotations is Dahrendorf's view that Marx can be described as the founder of the 'radical school'. Dahrendorf finds Marx's argument in Volume III of *Capital* to be a 'strange analysis' (1959, p. 22), but the explanation for this is that Dahrendorf has only taken note of a part of Marx's exposition. For while Marx did envisage the disappearance of the 'really functioning capitalist' and his supercession by 'mere managers', he also argued that these managers would consequently become subject to the representatives of a new predatory 'finance capitalism'. This thesis has been developed further by Marxists such as Aaronovitch (1961).

shareholders and have considerable holdings themselves. Interlocking directorships therefore ensure a representation of these interests in business enterprises.

(iii) Even if top managers are not large owners of business property in relation to the total shareholding in a big company, the actual and potential value of their own holdings may be quite a large proportion of their personal wealth and may even supplement their income quite considerably. For this reason alone they are unlikely to pursue policies detrimental to business ownership.

(iv) Even if senior managers do not possess significant holdings of capital, they are still likely to share similar aspirations and values with large shareholders as a result of sharing a similar social background and the respect for property which it induces.

(v) Business enterprises having different concentrations of ownership are all subject to similar market constraints (the environing system of capitalism), which means that severe limits are set to the choice of policies which their controllers can adopt in any case. For instance, the management of an enterprise which neglected its shareholders' interests would expose itself to the sanction of a take-over, which has become increasingly threatening with modern sophisticated stock market analysis (cf. Marris, 1964, 1967).

For these various reasons, the Marxist school holds that top managers and major capital-owners are not distinct groups in any sociologically important respect. Managers do not therefore comprise either a new elite or a new independent technocratic group, both of which have been claimed by managerialist writers. In short, the development of management does not signify an important modification of traditional social stratification (Mills, 1956; Barratt-Brown, 1958–9; Samuel, 1960; Aaronovitch, 1961; Villarejo, 1961–2; Blackburn, 1965; Westergaard, 1965; Baran & Sweezy, 1966; Miliband, 1968).

Neither set of managerialist writings presents so consistent or homogeneous an exposition as does the Marxist school. Among the sectional managerialists, the best known work is James Burnham's *The Managerial Revolution* (1941), while the most impressive analyses have come quite recently from 'managerial economists'. The chief interest of Burnham's book lies in its role as popularizer of the managerialist viewpoint. But as a contribution to serious scholarship it has rightly been severely criticized for inconsistent, over-simplified and spurious argument as well as for incorrect prediction (Bendix, 1945; Gerth & Mills, 1952; Dahren-dorf, 1959, pp. 87–91). Burnham's thesis was, in brief, that managers would emerge as a new ruling class within the cor-porate state towards which Stalinism, Nazism and the New Deal all signified a movement. Because managers performed indispensable bureaucratic functions and had access to the means of production, Burnham assumed *ipso facto* that they would inevitably be able to exercise power in their own interests.

In the main, managerial economists have followed the classical model of economic man in assuming that managers will act rationally so as to serve their own best interests. How-ever, their acceptance of the conclusion that ownership is divorced from control poses the question of how managerial self-interest will be expressed. Some hold that this will remain in a form which comes close to profit-maximization (Earley, 1957; Baldwin, 1964). Others suggest that the need for profits merely acts as a restraint on managers' attempts to maximize other variables which can fulfil more important functions for them—such as sales revenue (Baumol, 1959), growth of assets (Marris, 1964), or long-run profits and growth (Penrose, 1959). Gordon (1961) implied that managerial controllers would seek to maximize a utility function in terms of some combina-tion of financial and non-pecuniary rewards. Williamson's recent contribution (1964) is based on a comparable assump-tion, as is Galbraith's in *The New Industrial State* (1967) where he also assumes that the relative importance of pecuniary rewards diminishes as one moves up managerial hierarchies. Cyert and March (1963) argue that managers working within a framework of imperfect knowledge and uncertainty will in practice seek to achieve a 'satisfactory' rather than theoretically maximum level of return. With the notable exceptions of Gordon and Galbraith, economists have tended to show less concern than sociologists over the possible social consequences of self-interested managerial control in larger enterprises. Sociologists such as A. M. Rose (1967) assert that managers have been systematically exploiting their powers at others' expense, while those such as Moore (1962) certainly fear that this can happen.

The non-sectional managerialists take a more optimistic view. They have felt that because managers appeared to be enjoying conditions in which they did not have to maximize returns to ownership—a sectional interest—they could now pursue policies which reflected a more balanced set of goals in terms of meeting a wide range of social as well as economic requirements. This has long been the claim of management theorists (Child, 1969), and it was the hope of Tawney and Veblen as well as of Berle and Means who wished managerial control to 'develop into a purely neutral technocracy, balancing a variety of claims by various groups in the community and assigning to each a portion of the income stream on the basis of public policy rather than private cupidity' (1932, p. 356). Berle, though very aware of the political dangers in concentrated economic power, has more recently come to believe that managers do in the main follow the dictates of their 'corporate conscience' which is itself founded on an appraisal of public opinion backed by the threat of governmental or legal intervention (1954; 1957; 1959a). Such is the model of the 'soulful corporation' (Kaysen, 1957).

There are several other strands of non-sectional managerialism. The 'human relations' approach among management theorists and social scientists posited a social mission for managers of reviving within the enterprise the web of satisfying social relationships which 'industrialization' had destroyed in the wider society (Mayo, 1933, 1945; Whitehead, 1936). Some human relations writings implied that managers were in fact meeting this social challenge. Drucker in his earlier writings (1943; 1946; 1951) agreed with the human relations view that the business enterprise represented a viable community in its own right. This community had to operate in harmony with the rest of society, which meant that management had to accept prevailing societal values (a view comparable to that of Parsons, 1952; 1956). However, managers also faced a problem of legitimizing their authority within the enterprise because of the separation from ownership, and Drucker proposed that this should be secured by a limited extension of employee decision-making within what he saw (with considerable exaggeration) as a new 'self-governing plant community'. Some right-wing British labour intellectuals, notably Crosland (1956; 1962) and Strachey (1956) have accepted Berle's point of view, and have concluded in effect that socialist objectives have been achieved in industry through the passing of business control to socially-minded managers. All these non-sectional managerialists share the assumption of a potential harmony between managerial and social objectives consequent on the divorce of ownership from control.

In this last respect, Dahrendorf (1959) represents a definite exception. While he can be classed as a non-sectional managerialist in that he believes the separation of ownership and management to promote different outlooks (and more socially conscious ones on the part of management), Dahrendorf argues that this separation has had only limited import for social conflict and stratification. For Dahrendorf, class and class conflict in modern society is based primarily on relationships of authority rather than of property.

The debate over the nature and social implications of ownership and control relationships in modern large business enterprises has been confused for reasons which Nichols identifies (1967, Section 5). First, it has been conducted in the absence of sufficient empirical data. Participants in the controversy have been forced to rely on inferences drawn from industrial and social structure. Second, as we noted earlier, the debate has been characterized by semantic confusion. Third, it is largely a political and polemical debate. And fourth, Marxist and managerialist protagonists follow different logics of analysis. The Marxist commences with an examination of social identities and interests, while the managerialist tends to limit his purview to assessing the probability of who controls a particular type of enterprise and of how far the controllers are constrained by the enterprise's immediate environment.

Those engaged in this controversy disagree as to the institutional basis for holding control within the business enterprise, and as to the nature of relationships between enterprises and environment. Property ownership plays a central role in traditional Marxist analysis as the source of socioeconomic power, while the managerialists emphasize officeholding. For Marxists, property ownership provides a means and motive for economic exploitation and hence the controllers of industry adopt a purely private definition of the business enterprise and its functions in society. The enterprise becomes a focal point of relationships between an exploiting and exploited class. The sectional managerialists also assume that business controllers will adopt a private definition of their functions—it is merely the source of control which has changed. There still exist conflicting interests between the new managerial controllers and other social groups, which now include owners. The non-sectional managerialists present a different interpretation. They assume that a managerial separation from ownership makes for the acceptance of a new definition of the business enterprise through which greater social harmony can be achieved. They see managers as able to balance various economic and social objectives in a composite assessment of business responsibilities which approximates to what we shall call a 'social', as opposed to a 'private', definition of business.

4 DIVORCE OF OWNERSHIP FROM CONTROL—SOME EVIDENCE

The managerialist case relies on two main arguments. First, that a proportionately minute shareholding possessed by senior managers is evidence of their separation from ownership. Second, that a low concentration of voteholdings among the few largest shareholders in an enterprise makes it likely that the incumbent managers will also have effective control over policy.

Berle and Means employed this purely 'mechanical criterion' (Gordon, 1961, p. 166n) of the concentration of voteholdings among 'a compact group of individuals' (meaning up to about three shareholders) to find that of the 200 largest US non-financial corporations in 1928–30, 44% appeared to be 'management controlled' with no dominant stock interest known to exceed 5% (1932; Chapter V). Gordon (1961), using data for large US non-financial corporations during 1937–9, confirmed Berle and Means' findings, but warned that these did *not* give much indication of the extent to which ownership groups actually shared in business control. He therefore complemented these results with a detailed study of 'business leadership' in 65 very large corporations, concluding that full-time 'professional managers' *did* normally exercise control and had not usually achieved their position through share-ownership. More recently Larner (1966) repeated Berle and Means' study for the 200 largest US non-financial corporations in 1963, finding that virtually all these could now be classed as 'management-controlled'. In England, Florence (1961) examined in detail 268 of the larger public joint-stock companies over the period 1936–51. Applying more rigorous mechanical criteria than Berle and Means, he concluded that about two-thirds of the larger English companies (with assets over £200,000) were probably not owner controlled in 1951, and that from 1936 to 1951 there was a clear trend towards a greater divorce of ownership from control in very large companies.

Despite this weight of evidence, other researchers using somewhat different mechanical criteria have come to the conclusion that, in the United States at least, the separation of ownership from control is by no means as complete as is generally assumed (Villarejo, 1961–2; Kolko, 1962; Cheit, 1964). More important still is the fact that the Berle-Means methodology is completely inadequate for the thesis which has been constructed upon it, as Beed has well argued in an important critique (1966). Even at the level of an individual enterprise, Berle and Means' type of evidence could be used just as readily to support the view that the majority of minute shareholders were disfranchised leaving those with even a few per cent of the votes in positions of influence. And their attempt to extend their argument to the capitalist system as a whole was quite unwarranted without a consideration of prevailing social structure. Moreover, as both Beed and Allen (1967; p. 12) have pointed out, investigations into ownership and control have been confined to large enterprises and their already ambiguous results can certainly not be extrapolated to the total economic system.

There are two further qualifications to add to the mechanical analyses of ownership and control. First, in recent years a growing proportion of industrial shareholdings have come into the ownership of financial institutions such as insurance companies, pension funds, investment trusts and unit trusts. In Britain, insurance companies account for the greater part of this investment which has risen steadily from 18% of all quoted ordinary shares (in 1957) to 24–25% (end of 1963), reaching 32% at the close of 1966 (Blease, 1964; Revell & Moyle, 1966; Fry, 1968). Since financial institutions tend to concentrate their investments on the most promising companies, the percentage of shares they hold in any one enterprise may be well above the average figure. Most commentators have argued that financial institutions are more interested in securing a good rate of return on their investments rather than in exercising control by virtue of their ownership rights (e.g. Berle, 1959; Lintner, 1959), and insurance associations themselves make the same point (cf. *The Times* 28/5/1962). However, others have pointed out that institutional intervention over company policies has become more frequent (Johnson, 1967), and may be more extensive than is generally realized since it is normally kept secret (Fry, 1968). In this current development, then, we have a potential, if not actual, reversal of the divorce between ownership and control.

Second, the Berle-Means type of analysis overlooked the point that while a senior manager may own an insignificant proportion of his company's shareholdings, this ownership can still represent a considerable investment for him personally, and hence assume importance as an influence on his behaviour. Reworking Florence's data for 1951, Nichols found that among 89 large companies, the nominal value of the average directorial shareholding was £20,719, although this high figure did rest on the very great holdings of a few directors (1967, Section 6). Recent investigation in the United States also indicates that the controllers of industry are still frequently owners of fairly considerable business property in absolute terms. Stock-option schemes encourage this personal shareholding (Cheit, 1964, pp. 178–9). These facts lend some support to the Marxist view that a significant identity of interest remains between top managers and shareholders in modern capitalist industry. Further, a review of the available, but scanty evidence on top managers' socialization patterns both before and after joining the business enterprise, led Nichols to conclude that non-propertied and propertied company directors were likely to share the same general value orientations and to enjoy common social relationships. Both types of top manager tend to have far more in common than with other groups in the enterprise (1967, Sections 10, 11 & 12).

The relative strengths of the Marxist and managerialist schools may be tested by reference to further empirically observable criteria. For example, are the ideologies expressed by managers today appreciably different to those associated with the heyday of the owner-entrepreneur? Or to take a more direct indicator, do the policies pursued by managers appear to differ significantly according to the ownership-control situation in enterprises as measured by mechanical criteria?

Nichols has commented that the Berle-Means expectation of a 'neutral technocracy' developing from a supposed managerial freedom from ownership control possessed considerable ideological potential (1967, p. 24). Dahrendorf (1959) associated a new business ideology with a divorce of ownership from control because of the changed basis of managerial legitimation that had arisen. There is no question that during the course of this century, a managerial ideology stressing the responsible social role of managers towards groups within and outside the enterprise has been much in evidence, and that this ideology has often been explicitly linked to the idea of a divorce from ownership (cf. Bendix, 1956; Walton, 1967 for the American case, and Child, 1969 for the British). Moreover, as Walton indicates in his excellent review of the arguments for and against the notion of business social responsibilities, business spokesmen in recent years have been primarily among its advocates, while its foremost opponents have belonged to other groups—liberal economists like Friedman (1963), philosophers like Hayek (1960), business school academics like Levitt (1958), or lawyers like Rostow (1959). This marked difference seems to add some plausibility to the argument that the trend towards a formal separation of ownership and management has encouraged a redefinition of business responsibilities from a purely private towards a social conception—as the non-sectional managerialists claim.

Yet it would be unwise to conclude that a lack of managerial property-ownership was the prime factor behind the new managerial ideology, or indeed that this ideology necessarily expressed the views of practising managers. Socially oriented policies specifically decrying a narrow concentration on profit-maximization as the prime business objective, were expressed forcefully by some owner-employers (especially those with strong religious affiliations) before the main development of managerial ideology, or even before management had on any scale emerged as a distinct occupational grouping (Child, 1964). Second, a study of the progress of management thought during this century suggests that the relative weight given to a social definition of business objectives varied primarily according to the strength of censure which was in different respects directed towards management. And third, there is evidence that management ideology was in any case the product of intellectual spokesmen for management rather than an expression of the deep-felt views of most managers themselves (Child, 1968, 1969). Nichols found in his study of senior managers in a northern English city, that when asked about 'socially responsible' policies, the majority of these managers approved of such policies because they represented the most *practically* effective courses of action in modern socio-economic conditions (1967, Part III). American evidence also supports this finding (e.g. Harvard Business Review, 1961, p. 10; General Motors statement reported by Long, 1959). In short, the expression of support for a social definition of business responsibilities would appear to result from factors other than just the ownership position of top managers; factors such as religious values, the general socio-economic climate surrounding business and possibly the intellectual backgrounds of managerial spokesmen themselves.

Attitudes and ideologies, though easier to ascertain, are at best only uncertain guides to actual behaviour. Many of the managerialist predictions on the consequences of a separation between ownership and control have concerned the different objectives and policies which the new controllers would pursue. Two predictions have been fairly precisely stated: (i) that the 'managerial enterprise' would pursue objectives other than the maximization of profit assumed to be the primary goal of the classical owner-managed firm; (ii) that managers separated from ownership would distribute the earnings of a business enterprise in such a way as to minimize payments to shareholders, maximize plough-back, and thereby secure (directly or indirectly) rewards desirable to themselves (a sectional managerialist view).

(i) The evidence available on profit-maximization suggests that the managerialist view is deficient on two counts. First, the conventional notion that owner-entrepreneurs maximized their profits assumes both perfect knowledge of all possible alternatives (which was clearly untrue), and that these entre- preneurs were themselves such a different species of man that they too could not find any value in those objectives which have been ascribed to manager-controllers, ranging from the desire for a 'quiet life' to the desire that business operations should benefit as many other people as possible. There is little foundation for either of these assumptions, and indeed the modern large corporation employing sophisticated manage- ment techniques may be in a far better position actually to maximize profits than ever the classical entrepreneur was (Baran & Sweezy, 1966, Chapter 2).

Second, what research we have on large (American) cor- porations strongly suggests that at least the more successful ones do pursue the highest profits attainable within their knowledge of alternative strategies in respect of the surround- ing environment (Earley, 1957; Baldwin, 1964). In other words, within the limits of Simon's 'bounded rationality' (1947)—which improved techniques are steadily pushing out- wards—managers appear quite typically to pursue policies aimed at profit maximization, which in any case they do not see as seriously inconsistent with other financial objectives. The available evidence implies that we should be quite clear in distinguishing between managerial intentions (which may remain oriented towards profit-maximization) and actual managerial performance which may well depart from a theoretical profit-maximizing optimum.

(ii) Florence (1961) examined the ratios of distributed to retained profits in his sample of large English companies, and claimed to find a positive association between his measures of low ownership control and low divided distribution (high % of profits retained). However, Nichols (1967) reworked Florence's data for very large companies in the sample (those with assets of £3 million or over) and found that while the results were in the direction asserted by Florence, none reached a 5% level of significance. Lintner (1956, 1959) found in a detailed investigation of 28 large US companies that dividend policies had remained remarkably stable over long periods of time. This finding does not support a mana- gerialist view that dividend policies should have been sensi- tive to changes in the relation of management to ownership (cf. Berle & Means, 1932, Chapter VI). Lintner indeed concludes more generally that most of Berle and Means' predictions regarding the financial behaviour of apparently managerially-controlled firms have failed to materialize in the USA, and that corporations have not become free of various constraints imposed by the capital market (1959, p. 190). Allen (1967, p. 19) suggests that in any case most industrial firms have always grown by means of ploughing back profits, while Nichols (1967, Section 9) cites various evidence indicating a considerable overlap in the interests, and consequent financial behaviour, of both business owners and managers.

It is also worth noting that the thesis of diverging managerial and shareholder interests leads easily to the assumption that the interests of shareholders themselves are alike. Baran and Sweezy have argued convincingly that the interest of large shareholders is allied to a managerial interest in low-dividend payouts because of taxation considerations which do not apply in the same degree to small shareholders (1966, Chapter 2, Section 5). The course of some take-over deals in Britain further suggests that shareholders' interests are by no means all alike (cf. *The Times* 17/7/68 on American Tobacco's bid for Gallahers). All in all, the weight of evidence again indicates that the implications of a differentiation between ownership and control have been exaggerated by the managerialist school.

Finally, does the extent to which ownership and control are differentiated have any apparent effect upon the organizational structure of business enterprises? Hinings *et al.* (in a paper to appear) report the relationships found between the ownership/control position of 33 business organizations in Birmingham (measured primarily in terms of concentration of vote-holdings) and various features of their management structure. The only structural aspect which appeared to be affected by ownership and control was the degree to which decisions on important matters affecting the whole organization were centralized. Some association was found between the concentration of voteholding and the centralization of such decision-making, though this finding was based on a sub-sample of only 11 organizations.[4]

[4] Interest in the ownership and control issue has derived from the possible implications for the content of business objectives rather than

In short, the popular managerialist thesis that the separation of business ownership and control is one of the most momentous developments in modern capitalist society fails to remain convincing when placed alongside the available evidence. This evidence suggests instead that in such society there are wider economic, social and technological constraints operating on the business enterprise which tend to minimize the behavioural differences between owner-managers and non-propertied managers. This is not to say that the alternative Marxist thesis can therefore be accepted uncritically. This, too, makes some oversimplified assumptions regarding, for example, the range of objectives held by owner-managers or the deterministic importance of property ownership *per se*.

The Marxist and managerialist schools of thought share a concern for the way in which those in control of business might use their power, and an interest in the means whereby that power may be held to account. Indeed, the fact that many businessmen seem to acknowledge the concept of social responsibility because it pays them to do so in contemporary social climates, really indicates how in the absence of other controls the restraints upon the use of their substantial powers would be quite slender. In practice, it has for this reason been felt necessary in all modern industrial societies to impose external restrictions on the exercise of business power so that this should accord more closely with generally accepted social values. The imposition of this social definition of business has come primarily from government.

5 EXTERNAL CONTROL OVER THE BUSINESS ENTERPRISE

Cheit (1964) has concluded that the cultivation of social responsibility by American managers represents their conservative response to a changing business environment in which threats of greater public and governmental pressures are being felt. Berle (1954) also argued that 'corporate conscience'

---

for the nature of formal structure. There seems no *prima facie* reason to expect that different ownership/control patterns will greatly affect organizational structure except in so far as managerial controllers might (if one accepts the non-sectionalist managerialist thesis) modify that structure in order to try and promote social objectives such as the enhancement of employee satisfaction and welfare.

was imposed primarily by the force of public opinion and threats of governmental intervention. Similarly, it is likely that one of the reasons why even non-propertied managers continue to appeal to the sanctity of private property, and indeed more generally to the notion of 'managerial prerogatives', is in order to maintain their freedom from external controls and political interference (Gordon, 1961, p. 341; Mason, 1959, p. 11).

Nevertheless, despite these ideological defences, quite considerable controls are imposed upon the operation of business enterprises in modern industrial societies. These externally imposed controls contrast with the notion of social responsibility, which implies a voluntary and somewhat diffuse willingness of those directing a business enterprise to abide by, and perhaps actively enhance, socially approved practices. External, 'involuntary' control on business enterprise has been discussed primarily in terms of two concepts—first, the idea of 'countervailing power' and second, the concept of 'accountability'.

Galbraith developed the thesis of countervailing power in his analysis of *American Capitalism* (1952), and it has been applied particularly to capitalist societies where direct governmental regulation of business is less evident than in a communist society. Galbraith's argument was that 'private economic power is held in check by the countervailing power of those who are subject to it' (1952, p. 125). Countervailing power develops in response to a concentration of business power, as oligopsony might develop as a bargaining counter to oligopoly. The countervailing power concept is encompassed by the popular pluralist model of modern western societies. This portrays a distribution of power among a variety of groups or institutions in society, thus permitting a balance of power between different interests and preventing the dominance of any single collection of interests in any matter at issue (among many pluralist interpretations of the distribution of power in modern society see Bell, 1961 and Lipset, 1963).

Accountability represents an important mechanism for the exercise of countervailing power. This concept refers to relatively specific requirements placed upon the business enterprise by external agencies whose powers in this respect are

typically backed by legal sanction. These requirements include the declaration of financial information, the auditing of
company accounts, and the stipulation of shareholders' rights.
In addition to the legal definition of business accountability
it is meaningful to distinguish quasi-legal requirements such
as those imposed by stock markets for companies wishing to
have their shares quoted. Thirdly, some accountability may
rest upon custom and convention such as the customary (and
now expected) practice of some boards of directors to disclose
more information to shareholders than they are legally required to do (Ennis, 1967).

In all modern industrial societies, capitalist and communist, the relationship between regulatory organs of the
state and business enterprises are controversial and involve
considerable bargaining (cf. Hodson, 1967). However, particularly in communist countries but also in capitalist ones,
the state is today capable and often willing to exert a very
considerable control over the business enterprise. In the
Soviet Union, for instance, the organs of regional government
allocate a detailed set of production targets to the enterprise
and, despite recent tentative steps towards greater enterprise
autonomy, these state bodies still normally specify the enterprise's suppliers, customers and prices. The system provides
for the actual operations of the enterprise to come under the
independent surveillance of party and trade union officials,
who themselves have the authority to report to higher state
authorities (Richman, 1965; Birman, 1968; Connock, 1968;
Nove, 1968a, 1968b, 1969). In western societies state controls
typically cover questions of monopoly and restrictive practices (Allen, 1968), working conditions (Wedderburn, 1965),
location, conditions of sale and recently in Britain matters
such as pricing, employee incomes and dividends, and racial dis-
crimination (for a general review of the British case see Grove,
1962). The statutory provisions governing British nationalized
industry represent a further form of state control (Tivey, 1966).
Apart from direct control, the ability of governments to influence business behaviour derives from their fiscal and mone-
tary powers of economic regulation, their massive support of
research and development programmes and contracts for the
products of science-based industries, and (in Britain at least)
the threat of a state take-over of particular enterprises.

Having outlined this apparently impressive range of countervailing measures against the social misuse of business power, there remains the important question sociologically of how effective these external controls really are in practice. Certainly, there are those who would doubt the effectiveness of countervailing power, especially in the American case to which the concept was first applied and where governmental economic regulation is relatively conservative (Mills, 1956; Bottomore, 1964; Westergaard, 1965). Among the instances where countervailing power does not operate effectively is a condition of inflation, under which business units can simply pass on increased costs to the consumer rather than bargaining among themselves for lower costs, incomes and prices. Although Galbraith himself recognized this as a limitation to his argument, it seriously challenges his whole thesis in that inflation has been the normal post-war condition of capitalist societies.

It is also argued by the critics of countervailing power that an examination of social plurality indicates how the senior decision-makers of many major institutions share a common social identity and may even possess extensive kinship ties (Mills, 1956; Lupton & Wilson, 1959; Guttsman, 1964). The chief institutional exception in this respect is the labour movement, which in Britain has succeeded through Labour governments in imposing a relatively comprehensive range of restrictions on the powers of private business (Crosland, 1959). However, in the United States the labour movement has been less able or willing to challenge business power outside a narrow micro-economic field, and it is on the admission of at least one of its spokesmen currently facing a serious decline in membership and bargaining power (Barkin, 1965). Even Galbraith in his recent analysis of the American *New Industrial State* (1967) has now apparently reached the conclusion that countervailing power, from whatever quarter, against big business has seriously broken down.[5]

There are, then, some grounds for treating the thesis of countervailing power with caution, and the same warning is appropriate regarding the efficacy of governmental control over business enterprise. For example, Bernstein (1955)

[5] We return to this controversial book in Chapter IV.

studied the history of American federal regulatory commis-
sions, and he came to the conclusion that these have in practice tended to operate more in the interests of the regulated
business groups than of the general public. Restrictive practices legislation in Britain has been challenged by an increase
in amalgamation between enterprises and by the use of
devices such as 'open price agreements' which until very
recently continued to be legal (Allen, 1968). The reliance of
governments upon business advice for the formulation and
implementation of legislation gives business an opportunity
to ensure informally that its interests are represented (Rogow
& Shore, 1955; Finer, 1956). Occasionally business pressures
may be sufficiently effective as to induce new legislation as
was the case with the introduction of commercial television
in Britain (Wilson, 1961). In the United States, anti-trust
legislation is not applied to many giant firms such as General
Dynamics.[6] Hacker agrees with Galbraith's recent view on
the American situation when he explains this as 'a harmony
of political forms and economic interests on a plane determined by the on-going needs of corporate institutions'
(Hacker, 1965, p. 11; Galbraith, 1967). Representatives of
British industry, such as the Director-General of the CBI,
have indeed expressed conditional approval of closer relations
between business and government so long as this arrangement is of mutual benefit (J. Davies, 1967).

In Soviet society, the 'on-going needs' of industrial enterprises also tend to undermine the procedures for state control
over business management. Managers feel obliged to indulge
in illegal practices particularly with respect to securing scarce
resources and affording information on productive capabili-
ties when bargaining for favourable planning quotas (Berliner, 1957; Granick, 1960; Richman, 1965). The new system
of economic regulation which is being adopted in the USSR
and in East European communist societies formally accepts
that managers are to be given greater authority over certain
expenditures, labour force composition and some other
matters (*Problems of Communism*, various 1966 issues; Bush,
1967; Nove, 1969).[7] In Yugoslavia there has been consider-

[6] The recent decision (January, 1969) to file an anti-trust suit against
IBM shocked the American business community.

[7] However, the Russian state authorities seem to have been very

able decentralization of decision-making down to the level of individual enterprises for some time now, coupled with an officially sponsored formal system of worker control designed to secure managerial accountability. However, the development of extensive worker control within enterprises has been retarded by a number of factors, and there is evidence suggesting that one of these factors is again the pressures imposed by everyday business operations—that is, by the enterprise as a 'working organization' (Riddell, 1968, especially pp. 62–9).

These events raise the general question of whether economic and technological forces involved in communist industrial development are encouraging a divorce between political control (representing an owning general public) and managerial control over industry. This presents an interesting parallel with the ownership and control debate in capitalist societies. Indeed, both issues are aspects of the wider and central sociological problem of whether economic development sets up overwhelming pressures towards similar configurations of business enterprise. We shall delay further consideration of this broader question until Chapter VI. What we can conclude at this stage is that modern industrial societies have a large stake in the continuing prosperity of business enterprises, especially those representing large aggregations of capital, employment and know-how. Therefore, the controllers of business enterprises, whose experience of industrial operations is not readily replaceable, enjoy an advantage in bargaining with state agencies for the securing of their private objectives rather than those of a wider social appeal.

6 DISCUSSION

The underlying theme of this chapter has been the power enjoyed by those in effective control of business enterprises by virtue of the concentration of economic resources at their disposal. The way in which such power is used is of great social concern. Not only do economic resources represent a considerable social investment, but equally the conditions under which business operates has a significant influence on the quality of life enjoyed by members of society both as

---

reluctant in practice to extend greater autonomy to enterprise managers even when the reforms prescribed this—see Frankel (1967).

producers and consumers. Thus business power constitutes an important aspect of the relations between the enterprise and its environment.

Interpretations of the so-called divorce of ownership from control in private capitalist industry have concerned its possible consequences for the exercise of business power, particularly for the way in which business controllers might regard their objectives and responsibilities. We concluded that available evidence tends to favour the 'Marxist' interpretation rather than the 'managerialist' ones, though it also shows this to be oversimplified. It is certainly clear that an uncritical acceptance of non-sectional managerialism, in terms of a neutral managerial technocracy willingly adopting a social definition of business, is not possible as a general rule. But if one cannot necessarily rely on the restraint of business power from within, neither do controls from without operate wholly effectively in capitalist or communist societies. It is for this reason that in recent years so much concern has been expressed over the issue of business power (see the American references given earlier, plus Anderson & Blackburn, 1965).

The objective assessment of how power is distributed in contemporary industrial society is one of the most difficult tasks facing the sociologist (Lockwood, 1964). The investigation of business power has rarely moved beyond an assessment of the power which could be imputed to given configurations of formal positions and statuses. Clearly one needs to move beyond this primarily mechanical analysis, though the practical difficulties of research in such a complex and sensitive area are severe. Nichols (1967) has listed a dozen examples of areas where sociological investigation has been insufficient and even non-existent. For example, more research is required on the actual processes of policy formation within the business enterprise; it is also important for sociologists to investigate the frames of reference and objectives of businessmen in enterprises with different ownership situations, allowing for independent factors such as size and industrial environment. As a starting point to such further investigation, the conceptualization and operationalization of power as a variable (or set of variables) must be taken to a more satisfactory level of development than is currently the case.

The attention given to social responsibility by business

E

spokesmen, the concern of many academics with the exercise of business power, and the increasing number of governmental measures to control business activity, all testify to a widespread acceptance in modern industrial societies that a purely private definition of business responsibility is inadequate. It is increasingly felt that the influence of business enterprises over matters of genuine social concern requires their performance to be assessed with some reference to social criteria. This movement of opinion reflects a changing sociocultural environment which now manifests greater expectations of business with respect to matters such as the quality of working conditions or security of tenure. It has also been encouraged by the development of social science research that has provided evidence of the social problems associated with business operations. The following chapter reviews some of this evidence in relation to rising social expectations.

CHAPTER IV

Social Problems of Modern Business Enterprise

This chapter examines some of the social problems associated with the policies and operations of business enterprises. The extent to which features of an enterprise themselves give rise to social problems has to be gauged in relation to the whole range of factors which help to shape the attitudes and behaviour that, in turn, suggest the presence of socially unsatisfactory conditions. An assessment of this kind will place us in a better position to examine, in the following chapter, the opportunities which are available for modifying the design of business enterprises so as to achieve more favourable social consequences without impairment to their economic effectiveness. The greater part of the present chapter is devoted to the quality of personal experience offered by business to its own employees at work. It also considers briefly how business activities can affect the quality of life enjoyed by people in their non-work roles, when they use their incomes for consumption or for the pursuit of leisure.[1]

1 QUALITY OF EXPERIENCE WITHIN THE ENTERPRISE—RELEVANT CONCEPTS

A person's '*quality of experience*' refers to the contribution which his various social roles make towards satisfying his goals

[1] We cannot here provide a comprehensive survey of research on the whole area of work experience, the sociology of leisure, or consumer behaviour. An introduction to the first two subjects is provided in Parker *et al.* (1968: part III); a thorough review of research on work experience in Vroom (1964); and a comprehensive collection of papers on consumer behaviour in Britt (1966).

and the needs of his personality. This is a matter to which some social scientists attach keen moral feelings, and the intrusion of these worthy sentiments should be quite clearly recognized and closely controlled for the sake of a reasonably objective analysis. Moreover, discussion about quality of experience demands reference to psychological as well as sociological modes of analysis, as a summary of relevant concepts and the interrelationships soon indicates.

Sociological concern about people's quality of experience at work has centred primarily on the complex concept of *'alienation'*. Although the alienation of modern man is a general theme running through the art, drama and literature of the western world, the term has been used to describe an extraordinary variety of psycho-social disorders and it has been applied to a wide range of different social groups (E. & M. Josephson, 1962, pp. 10–13). The thesis of alienation formed part of Marx's critique of the excessive division of labour in capitalist society. Marx argued that this caused the worker to lose control over the conditions and the fruits of his labour and led him to experience estrangement both from himself and his fellow-men (Bottomore & Rubel, 1956, Part 3, Section IV). Veblen considered the 'instinct of workmanship' to be a universal trait in man, and he associated the predominant role of business enterprise in western society with a financial manipulation of industry in terms of prices and costs detrimental to workmanship (Veblen, 1914). Marx and Veblen thus regarded alienation as a consequence of the capitalist economic system. Weber, however, linked alienating tendencies with bureaucratization, which he envisaged as a structural concomitant of any developed industrial society. He regarded the separation of employees from the means of production as just a particular case which had to be placed aside a similar development within government administration, the military, the universities, and so on (Gerth & Mills, 1946, pp. 49–50, Chapter VIII).

It is necessary to distinguish between (i) environing social conditions which may contribute towards alienation ('alienating conditions');[2] (ii) the interaction between environing

---

[2] These conditions have been emphasized in the social diagnosis of 'alienation' advanced by writers such as Marx (1844) and Marcuse (1964).

conditions and human requirements,[3] which may, if conflictual, form a role that is alienated ('alienated role'); and (iii) the subjective experience of individuals who are alienated ('experienced alienation'). Most attempts to define alienation and to isolate its components have focussed upon the subjective feeling of being 'estranged from' an institution, from a culture or even from society in general. The most influential paper on alienation is that by Seeman (1959) which attempted to separate out and classify five different meanings that have been given to the concept in the sociological literature: (i) powerlessness; (ii) meaninglessness; (iii) normlessness; (iv) self-estrangement (a lack of present-time involvement when behaviour becomes primarily instrumental towards anticipated future rewards); and (v) isolation, both physical and social. Newton (1968, Chapter X) has argued that Seeman's exercise does not bring us any nearer to a resolution of what alienation can most usefully be taken to mean. In his review of the literature, Newton clearly exposes the confusion which has existed in sociology over the definition of alienation and its relationship with allied concepts such as 'anomie', 'competence' and 'marginality'. This conceptual confusion has impeded an adequate operationalization of alienation for research purposes (Neal and Rettig, 1967 represent an important advance here), and this is in marked contrast to the operational progress which has been made with the more limited concept of job satisfaction.

An alienated role is a function of alienating conditions in conflict with personal requirements. The latter when applied to the former induce a consequent experience of alienation. Personal requirements may in part be represented by consciously experienced expectations and goals, and these have been conceptualized in terms of an *'orientation to work'*. Sociologists who focus upon the 'action' element in social processes, regard orientation to work (the ordered expectations and goals an individual has regarding the work situation) as a factor mediating between the objective features of the environing work situation and employees' subjective ex-

---

[3] Writers on alienation normally regard these human requirements as something more akin to basic needs than merely to conscious expectations which, of course, may not encompass the fulfilment of all a person's needs. However, there is considerable confusion on this particular point.

perience of, and reaction to, that situation (Goldthorpe, 1966, pp. 239–40; Silverman, 1968a). Thus, to return to alienation, objectively the same environing conditions within a business enterprise could promote an alienating work role for one employee who held a particular prior orientation to work, but not for another employee with a different orientation. Smith (1968) has added to the conceptualization of orientation to work by distinguishing between an employee's '*self-identity*' (shaped by socialization, personality development and similar) and his '*work-identity*' (shaped by self-identity in relation to the expectations of workplace reference groups). The latter corresponds to the employee's normative definition of his work situation (cf. Hopper, 1965). In Smith's analysis, how employees interpret their work roles is seen to be a function of 'objective structure' (such as technology) and work identity. Their interpretation of work roles can be assumed to influence employees' attitudes and behaviour.

The psychological approach to quality of work experience has generally centred on an analysis of '*need-satisfaction*' in relation to different features of the work-situation. Maslow's concept (1943, 1954), in which an individual's various needs are placed in a hierarchy of prepotency with self-actualization as the highest need, has been employed widely by writers such as Argyris (1957, 1960, 1962, 1964), who is concerned with the area of conflict between organizational and individual requirements. The applicability of the need-hierarchy concept to all employees has, however, been seriously questioned by recent research indicating that the relative importance of various needs (as expressed by employees' work values) differs between occupational levels (Friedlander, 1965, 1966; Centers & Bugental, 1966; Hall & Nougiam, 1968) and as between varying family backgrounds (Paine *et al.*, 1967). The broader implications for the individual of his need-satisfaction at work have been studied, using a multidimensional concept of '*mental health*' (Jahoda, 1958), by social psychologists such as Gurin *et al.* (1960, Chapter VI), French and Kahn (1962), and A. Kornhauser (1962, 1965). A further factor, which psychologists have generally associated with effective self-actualization, is expressed by the concept of '*involvement*' in work. Parker has suggested that work involvement has three aspects: (1) the degree of meaning attached to work; (2) the degree of identification with work; and (3) the degree to which work is a central life interest (Parker *et al.*, 1968, pp. 152–5).[4] Defined in this manner, involvement approximates to the antithesis of 'experienced alienation'.

More studies on the quality of work experience have centred on the concept of *'job satisfaction'* than any other. Unlike the study of alienation, where a concern for the dignity and freedom of man tends to be uppermost, the study of job satisfaction has often been motivated by a search for higher productivity in which regard for the individual has been relegated to the level simply of maintaining contentment. This point may be kept in mind during our subsequent review of available research, most of which has related to the job satisfaction concept. Although job satisfaction is a more closely contained concept than alienation, and has been operationalized fairly successfully, it has nonetheless also suffered from considerable definitional confusion. Parker (1964) has reviewed the main sources of this confusion. As with alienation, the object of satisfaction has not always been clearly identified.[5] The frames of reference adopted for research have differed considerably in breadth, and there has therefore been no generally accepted standard form for testing job satisfaction. There has also been a dispute as to whether job satisfaction is a unitary concept—'generalized job satisfaction' or 'morale'—or multidimensional, though recent research has tended to support the latter view (e.g. Handyside & Speak, 1964).

It is important to recognize that job satisfaction is a function of the relation between expectations and rewards (Morse, 1953), rather than of the relation between possibly more fundamental human requirements and the whole range of environing conditions in the workplace. For this reason, as Mills (1963, p. 86) and Wilensky (1966) have pointed out, there is not necessarily any direct correspondence between (i) the degree of experienced alienation or the extent to which

---

[4] See also Dubin's seminal study of employees' central life interests (1956).

[5] One problem is that the term 'job' does not have a single, unambiguous meaning. For instance, it can refer either to a specific work task, to a work role, or to employment generally.

given needs are satisfied, and (ii) the degree of measured job satisfaction. For instance, Goldthorpe (1966, 1968) has produced evidence that where high intrinsic rewards are not readily obtainable at work, some types of employee may still be willing to enter this work situation and use its favourable extrinsic rewards as an 'instrument' towards the gratification of their needs in the non-work sphere. In this case, some satisfaction may be derived from their jobs even though the work itself is of a potentially alienating nature and psychologically unfulfilling.[6] What is not yet known is whether a low intrinsic quality of work life would eventually impair mental health, despite high compensating extrinsic rewards. This is a most important social corollary of business operations which requires much further investigation.

2 QUALITY OF EXPERIENCE WITHIN THE ENTERPRISE—A PSYCHO-SOCIOLOGICAL MODEL

Most available studies relating to the quality of work experience have focussed on job attitudes (particularly expressed as job satisfaction) and on workplace behaviour (again with a heavy emphasis on satisfaction-related indices such as rates of absence, grievances, or labour turnover). A diagrammatic presentation serves usefully to order a review of these studies, and to indicate the relationship between some of the concepts just listed. Figure 1 therefore presents a model of quality of experience within the business enterprise, the form of which has been influenced both by the analyses of sociologists such as Goldthorpe (1966, 1968) and Smith (1968) to which we have already referred, and also the thinking of social psychologists such as Katzell, Barrett and Parker (1961, especially p. 65).

[6] A good predictor of overall job satisfaction is the degree to which those needs which employees rate highest are gratified (Schaffer, 1953; Froelich & Wolins, 1960; Haire *et al.* 1966; Payne, 1968). Thus in a work situation where only Maslow's lower order needs (physiological, security) were being satisfied by means of extrinsic rewards, the consequent effect on job satisfaction would depend on employees' own conscious assessment of their personal need priorities. We have already referred to research which indicates that these priorities are to a large degree socially rather than individually determined, and the nature of these social determinants is explored further in a following section on 'environmental determinants'.

FIGURE I—A model of variables influencing quality of experience within the business enterprise as indicated by job attitudes and behaviour

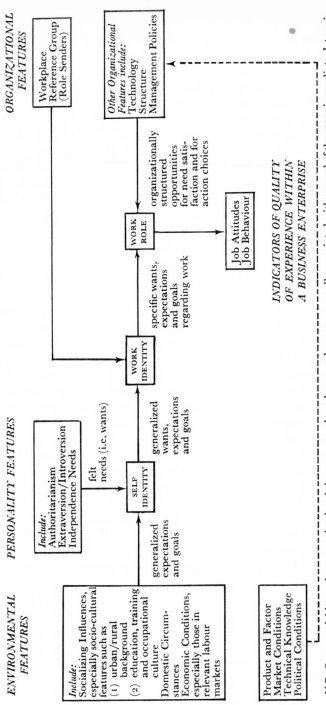

N.B. Some variables such as organizational size or an employee's age and sex are normally associated with several of the more immediate determinants shown in this diagram. They are omitted in order to preserve a simple presentation, but are discussed further at various points in the text.

The focal point of this model is the work role, which is the locus of interaction between (A) organizational characteristics (specifically, an organizationally structured set of demands, opportunities, pressures, and rewards) and (B) the individual's ordering of wants and expectations in relation to the work situation (work identity). This formulation immediately raises an important question which Vroom discusses (1964, pp. 161–5), namely whether attitudes and behaviour promoted by the work role are a function of the *difference* between (A) and (B), or of the *product* of (A) and (B). Available evidence is not conclusive, but Vroom thinks that it tends to support the second alternative.[7]

3 QUALITY OF EXPERIENCE WITHIN THE ENTERPRISE—SOME EVIDENCE ON DETERMINANTS

This section reviews research on determinants of job attitudes and behaviour and it follows Figure 1 by categorizing these as organizational, environmental and personality features.

A *Organizational Determinants*

The *technology* of a business enterprise has been accorded considerable attention as a determinant of employee attitudes and behaviour, sometimes to the exclusion of other relevant factors as critics such as Pugh (1966) and Goldthorpe *et al.* (1968) have pointed out. Vroom (1964, pp. 126–50) has brought together research which indicates that dissatisfaction at work can result from various features of '*micro technology*' (the techniques applied to individual tasks), such as extreme specialization and repetitiveness, lack of control over work methods or over the pace of work, and insufficient scope for the exercise of personal skills and abilities. The '*macro technology*' (the overall ordering of tasks) which generally represents the heaviest concentration of such task attributes is mass production, and this type appears to promote the greatest degree of alienation and dissatisfaction with work (cf. Walker & Guest, 1952; Chinoy, 1955; Woodward, 1958; Blauner, 1964). Sayles' research (1958) also indicates how the place of work groups within a production technology can

[7] Vroom's definition of work role is narrower than ours, and approximates to item (A) only.

affect important aspects of their behaviour. The interdependence of the technological with the social and economic dimensions of organization has been expressed in the important
concept of a '*socio-technical system*' (Emery & Trist, 1960;
Rice, 1963; Trist *et al.*, 1963).

There is as yet among researchers no extensive agreement
as to the relationship between organizational technology and
organizational structure (cf. Woodward, 1965; Harvey, 1968;
Hickson *et al.*, 1969), However, there is already considerable
evidence that certain features of organizational structure can
affect quality of work experience. Porter and Lawler (1965)
reviewing this evidence concluded that the strongest relationships were those associating a high position in the organizational hierarchy and membership of a small organizational
sub-unit (be this factory, department or even work group)
with a relatively high degree of job satisfaction.

Porter and Lawler did not find in their review that the
centralization or decentralization of decision-making was
systematically related to attitudes or behaviour. Their conclusion therefore does not positively support a view popular
in recent organization theory that the greatest degree of employee satisfaction and 'co-operative' behaviour at work will
be stimulated by a combination of technology and structure
that maximizes participative/decentralized decision making,
and job enlargement; and minimizes job routines or rules
which restrict individual initiative. This school of thought,
variously labelled 'neo-human relations', 'power-equalization'
and 'organizational democracy', generally accepts Maslow's
view that self-actualization represents the highest need for all
employees (cf. Argyris, 1957, 1960, 1962, 1964; McGregor,
1960; Likert, 1961, 1967). Studies by Friedlander (1965,
1966) and Centers and Bugental (1966), which we cited
earlier, suggest that opportunities for self-actualization at
work tend to be more highly valued by white-collar employees, and therefore by implication, that the neo-human relations approach to technology and structure may be more
appropriate to white-collar than manual jobs. A study by
Aiken and Hage (1966) suggests, further, that the neo-human
relations approach is appropriate (perhaps most so) to professional employees. For they found in sixteen welfare organizations that both alienation from work and from expressive

relations was most prominent in organizations that were highly centralized, and highly 'formalized' (relied heavily on the use of rules, had many codified jobs, and similar features).

The alienation of professional employees within bureaucratic organizations has become a major sociological interest in recent years.[8] The problem is one of growing dimensions since the numbers of these employees have been steadily increasing. The professional employee, such as the industrial scientist, the engineer or the company lawyer, has typically internalized a clearly defined set of norms which relate to his conduct. He tends to be strongly committed to his work, which he has attested technical competence to carry out. He has a strong self-identity deriving from professional socialization, and reinforced by professional membership, which gives him effective self-control over his occupational activities.[9] There is therefore a real conflict between this professional rationale and that of bureaucratic administration, primarily with respect to the professional desire for autonomy and the disciplined compliance with the orders and procedures deriving from administrative superiors which characterizes the bureaucratic control structure (Blau & Scott, 1962, p. 209; Hall, 1968). In short, if an individual has a strong professional identity, then the nature of the organizational framework within which he works may be a particularly keenly-felt influence upon his quality of experience.

Most research on the relation of *management policies* to quality of experience in the enterprise has concentrated on the more traditional human relations concerns of supervisory style and the integration of work groups. Several reviews of the many available research studies have concluded that employee-centred and participative supervisory styles[10] and

[8] Some of the most important studies and reviews are Abrahamson, 1967; Evan, 1962; Glazer, 1964; Hall, 1968; W. Kornhauser, 1962; Marcson, 1960; Miller, 1967; Orth *et al.*, 1965.

[9] In practice the strength of this 'professional' identity and the orientations it involves may vary among different professional groups (Becker & Carper, 1956; Shepherd, 1961; Box & Cotgrove, 1966).

[10] Participative supervision does not necessarily imply decentralized decision-making. First, participation may extend only to the determination of means and not of goals. Second, participation may not even extend to any determination at all, but may take the form merely of associating employees with decisions already taken (cf. Chapter V, pp. 89–92 below).

the social integration of work groups do typically appear related to high employee job satisfaction and a low propensity to absent or leave the enterprise (e.g. Argyle, 1957; Blauner, 1960; Vroom, 1964). However, there still remains some doubt as to the direction of causality in the case of supervisory style (Argyle, 1957, pp. 196–7; Vroom, 1964, pp. 112–3). In addition, a study by Pelz (1952) indicated that the effects of supervisory style on job satisfaction depended on the supervisor's own influence with his superior. Therefore supervision as a determinant of job satisfaction must be viewed in the context of the environing organizational structure, just as work group integration must be viewed in relation to the limits imposed by other organizational features such as technology and work group size.

Studies of supervisory style have nearly all been concerned with supervision over manual or clerical workers. There is, however, now some evidence suggesting that in the case of professional employees, particularly industrial scientists, it is not the participative style of supervision which affords them most satisfaction or least sense of alienation. Rather, they seem to prefer a *laissez-faire* style, one that gives them most autonomy and that leaves them to get on with their work as they see fit (cf. Miller, 1967). Here again the effect of supervisory policies have to be examined in relation to the wider context, in this case the occupational culture of the employees concerned.

In general, it is possible to deduce from our model (Figure 1) that any management policies which served better to reconcile opportunities offered by the enterprise with the expectations and wants of employees should thereby enhance their quality of experience at work.

The degree of social integration present in work groups is associated with the likely strength of common group norms. The effective strength of such norms will largely determine the importance which the work group assumes for the individual as a point of *workplace social reference*. Figure 1 postulates that workplace group norms can exert a significant influence on an employee's work identity, and hence on his response to other organizational conditions. This process has in fact been well illustrated by studies of employee output restriction (e.g. Roethlisberger & Dickson, 1939; Roy, 1952; Hickson, 1961; Lupton, 1963).

Organizational size is a factor which may be associated with several of the above organizational features, especially structure (Payne & Hickson, 1967; Pugh *et al.*, 1969). As Ingham (1967) has pointed out, both Marx and Durkheim put forward the thesis that the growth of large scale business enterprise heightened industrial conflict. More recently, positive correlations have been found between large organizational size and the incidence of strikes (Cleland, 1955; Revans, 1958, 1960), between large size and high absenteeism (Acton Society Trust, 1953, 1957; Indik, 1963, 1965), between large size and low overall job satisfaction (Talacchi, 1960) and between large size and low participation in organizational activities (Warner & Hilander, 1964). Porter (1963–4) carried out a series of studies into management attitudes which indicated that company size did affect managerial need satisfactions but that the relationship was mediated by the level of management in question. Thus top managers in larger companies and lower-level managers in smaller companies appeared more satisfied than did others.

Nevertheless, one cannot rest with the conclusion that it is large organizational size of itself which acts in these ways as a determinant of quality of experience. In the first place, it is possible for a business enterprise to grow to a large total size while retaining relatively small sub-units. Porter and Lawler (1965) concluded that sub-unit size was much more consistently related negatively to job satisfaction and positively to absenteeism and labour turnover than was overall organizational size (although one can quarrel with their broad definition of 'sub-unit' which included both work groups and whole factories!). Secondly, it is now widely recognized that the 'size-effect' operates via structural intermediaries. Weber, in his classic work on bureaucracy, felt that it was only the small organization that could avoid adopting bureaucratic characteristics (1947, p. 338). Both Indik and Talacchi have argued that the relationship between organizational size and low job satisfaction and symptoms of 'withdrawal' from the work situation is mediated by structural factors such as bureaucratization (including impersonal modes of control and role specialization), the relative amount of interpersonal communication possible in the organization, and strains towards functional autonomy and hence interdepartmental conflicts (Talacchi, 1960; Indik, 1963, 1965). Despite Ingham's argument to the contrary (1967, p. 242), the weight of available evidence does suggest a link between large size and both high specialization and other bureaucratic indices such as the use of impersonal control mechanisms (e.g. Hall and Tittle, 1966; Rushing, 1966; Hall *et al.*, 1967; Pugh *et al.*, 1969). Indik's research (1965) gave particularly strong support to the thesis that levels of interpersonal communication also represent a key intermediate factor. One returns at this point, of course, to the evidence we reviewed earlier which suggested the relevance for quality of work experience of specialization, routine, control, and work group social integration. In anticipation of the following chapter, it may be noted that the strength of the relationship between organizational size and other intermediate organizational variables has never been reported as being so high that considerable scope is not left for a modification of these other variables so as to promote greater personal satisfaction at work.

B *Environmental Determinants*

Organizational features do not account for all the variance found in quality of work experience within business enterprises, as this is manifested in job attitudes and behaviour. Brown (in Parker *et al.*, 1968, p. 118) refers to several studies which indicate considerable differences in satisfaction and behaviour in similar (though not precisely compared) technological situations (e.g. Bescoby & Turner, 1961; Guest, 1962; Goldthorpe, 1966).[11] Equally, it has been found that the manifestations of both technological and structural variables in similar task attributes has not necessarily resulted in similar levels of employee satisfaction or behaviour (Katzell *et al.*, 1961; Turner & Lawrence, 1965; Hulin & Blood, 1968). Nor have similar managerial policies, manifested in supervisory styles and opportunities for participation, always promoted similar levels of satisfaction or modes of behaviour (Vroom, 1964, pp. 105–19, 211–29). Although a knowledge

[11] More importantly in the case of the 'Luton Project', reported in Goldthorpe (1966) and Goldthorpe *et al.* (1968), very similar patterns of industrial attitudes and behaviour were found among manual workers employed in different technological settings.

of all these organizational characteristics taken together should permit a moderately successful prediction of employees' quality of work experience, this knowledge alone would fail to account for anywhere near the total picture. Thus a simple organizational determinism is inadequate, since the quality of employees' experience also depends in part upon social factors outside the compass of a business enterprise.

For instance, *socio-cultural features* (cf. Chapter II) play an important role in shaping the generalized goals and expectations of employees and managers. A number of studies have concluded that, in the context of American society at least, differences between membership of a city or large urban community, as opposed to a small town or rural one, are critical for an understanding of how employees experience their work situations. Turner and Lawrence (1965) found that job satisfaction in relation to task attributes varied considerably between predominantly Catholic city dwellers and predominantly Protestant small town/rural dwellers. This community differentiation also distinguished between attitudes to company and trade union. Earlier Katzell, Barrett and Parker (1961) had found that job satisfaction and performance was best predicted (in the case of 72 similar warehouses belonging to one company) by a series of factors—sex of employee, wage rate, degree of unionization and warehouse size—which were associated with location in a city as opposed to a small town. Hulin and Blood (1968), reviewing the literature on the relationship of job-enlargement to job satisfaction and behaviour, conclude that this depends to a large extent upon the socio-cultural backgrounds of employees. They argue that urban manual workers, who are likely to be alienated from middle-class work norms, are less likely to respond 'positively' to job enlargement than are white-collar workers or small town/rural manual workers (cf. also Karpik, 1966 for a French example of this urban/rural cultural difference). Form and Geschwender (1962) have reviewed other studies on job satisfaction and differential class perceptions of the occupational structure, as well as themselves studying over 500 Michigan manual workers. They conclude that job satisfaction in relation to occupational position depends on the individual's social reference group, be this working class without a strong internalization of the ideology of opportunity or middle class where this ideology is strongly held.

Levels of work satisfaction appear to be higher in those jobs where employees form a distinctive and close-knit occupational community both on and off the job (Blauner, 1960, p. 350). Mining and printing are examples. Moreover, the many findings of occupational differences in job satisfaction levels (cf. Lyman, 1955; Blauner, 1960; Parker, 1964) probably reflect not only differences in working conditions (an organizational feature), but also differences in occupational norms with respect to expectations of work. For instance, as a result of their training, professional employees have internalized standards of conduct and competence, and skilled workers have internalized standards of workmanship. Both groups therefore identify with, and are committed to their work and craft. Consequently, employees socialized within different occupational cultures may expect not only to enjoy different conditions of work but also to derive different degrees of satisfaction from that work (cf. Caplow, 1954, p. 133).[12] The influence of occupational culture may also help to explain Banks' finding (1963b) that the minority of workers in a British factory who expressed interest in various forms of participation were skilled (as well as older) men.

Finally, the influence of socio-cultural features on employee expectations (and hence eventually on their quality of experience at work) is confirmed by reference to cross-cultural international comparisons. Nath's (1968) valuable review of relevant research, cited in Chapter II, confirms the presence of such cross-cultural differences. Zurcher, Meadow and Zurcher (1965), studying Mexican, Mexican-American, and Anglo-American bank employees, found that their differing value orientations applied to a relatively standard work context predicted different degrees of alienation (measured, following Pearlin 1962, with a stress on powerlessness).

The sociological evidence on *economic factors* in a business environment as determinants of employee expectations is still

[12] The results of job satisfaction comparisons may be confounded by the likelihood that some employees (especially professional and some white-collar groups) will regard low job satisfaction as an admission of failure and therefore not admit this to investigators. Cf. Blauner (1960).

indirect, speculative, and *ex post facto* in nature. For example, Lupton (1963) suggests that his observed differences in worker behaviour at two British factories can be partly explained by reference to certain features of the enterprise environment, including the structure and behaviour of product markets, and the strength of union organization in the labour market. Siegel (1957) presents a cogent argument, and some supporting evidence, to the effect that employee attitudes and behaviour (particularly when manifested in industrial unrest) can only be understood adequately in terms of environing economic conditions. March and Simon (1958, pp. 58, 100–6) marshal evidence supporting the proposition that the individual's perception of alternative employments, which in turn may well influence his satisfaction with working for a given enterprise (Hulin, 1966), is partly influenced by the general level of business activity.

Finally, the economic requirements imposed by an individual's *domestic circumstances* (associated with his position in the life-cycle, styles of life, and so on) may influence his generalized expectations and thereby his orientation to work (Goldthorpe, 1966, p. 241). Shimmin (1962) has collected together some British research which indicates that domestic matters such as home ownership, patterns of expenditure on consumer durables, and number of dependents all influence employees' motivations to work, especially with respect to overtime. In Chapter II we cited Millward's study (1968) of young Lancashire female employees which illustrated how changes in their family status could bring about changes in their behaviour at work. In this context one may also mention the work of Paine and his colleagues (1967) who found that distinct patterns of family background were associated with different work values expressed by American college undergraduates.

C *Personality Determinants*

Our model of quality of experience in the enterprise postulates that self-identity will be influenced both by social environment and by an individual's personality characteristics. Although recognizing the likely relationship of social background to personality development, we are treating the two areas separately for purposes of clarity.

While it is outside our present brief to consider psychological variables in any detail, their independent contribution to the variance in quality of work experience must be recognized (cf. Pugh, 1966). For example, Vroom (1959, 1960) found that in a large American delivery company participation in decision-making had 'positive' effects on the attitudes and job performance of supervisors taken as a whole—this much is merely in line with the results of other studies. But Vroom was able, in addition, to demonstrate that the strength of these effects was a function of certain personality characteristics. For the opportunity to participate seemed to have little effect on the attitudes of persons who scored as *authoritarian* on the F scale (Adorno *et al.*, 1950) and who had weak *needs for independence*. Cooper and Payne (1967) refer to research suggesting the relevance of the *achievement need* and *acquiescence*, among other personality variables, to work behaviour. Their own study examined *extraversion* in relation to routine and repetitive packing work, and they found a correlation between the degree of extraversion and some behavioural indices such as non-permitted absence (positive) and length of service (negative). In this study, *neuroticism* also correlated positively with non-permitted absence, a finding supported by other previous research (cf. Herzberg *et al.*, 1957).[13]

The other area of social problems associated with the operation of modern business enterprise concerns the influence

[13] It is relevant to mention here two individual (though not, of course, personality) characteristics—*age* and *sex*. These characteristics may be associated with certain personality features. More importantly from the point of view of our present analysis, both age and sex are so closely associated with certain social positions and expectations that we can meaningfully speak of age and sex *roles*. For instance, age is commonly associated with various domestic circumstances (cf. the concept of 'life cycle'), while to both age and sex are attached certain social expectations about employment opportunities, career prospects and the like. Thus age and sex are variables which impinge upon several of the factors we have distinguished in our analytical scheme, and for this reason they can be regarded as indirect influences upon work attitudes and behaviour. (They have, for example, been found to correlate with level of job satisfaction, cf. Parker 1964.) We have, nevertheless, thought it less confusing to focus upon more direct influences in the main body of discussion.

which the larger firm in particular can exercise over the quality of people's lives outside the work situation. Indeed, to the extent that many employees may find little quality of experience at work, or possess an instrumental attitude towards work in any case, their 'central life interests' and opportunities to fulfil their whole range of psychological needs are limited to the non-work sector of their lives (Dubin, 1956; Cotgrove & Parker, 1963; Parker, 1965). They have, as Argyris (1958) has put it, signed a 'psychological work contract' exchanging satisfaction at work for a high wage to secure this elsewhere. Placed in this perspective, the influence of business over people's lives outside work, especially as income earners, consumers and leisure seekers, represents an issue of keen social concern.

4 QUALITY OF EXPERIENCE OUTSIDE THE BUSINESS ENTERPRISE

A *Income Distribution*

Gurin and his colleagues (1960) found that economic and material considerations were of prime importance in determining Americans' mental health. The critical function of the business enterprise for its membership groups is economic in the sense that, except under conditions of slavery, they would not lend their abilities to the enterprise without payment. The non-sectional managerialist model of obligations to a plurality of interests (see Chapter III) recognizes the distribution of income and rewards as a managerial responsibility in a capitalist economy. However, income distribution has in practice always formed a focus of conflict between those in control of business and other groups. The concepts of an 'effort-bargain' (Behrend, 1957) or a 'contributions-inducements balance' (Barnard, 1938; Simon, 1947) express the source of this conflict, namely the problem of what rewards should be offered for what individual contributions to the enterprise. We have suggested in the previous chapter that senior business managers may be induced to favour the interests of large shareholders rather than other claimants for income, and the widespread intervention in modern industrial societies of governments, trade unions, and financial institutions over matters of company payments signifies a feeling that businessmen cannot be trusted to pursue income distribution in accordance with socially defined values.

This distrust of business behaviour is reinforced by the findings that, despite relatively powerful trade unionism since the Second World War in Britain and the United States, and despite the public acceptance, in Britain at least, of an active role in income distribution by governments, there has been only a slight fall in overall income inequality in Britain since the Second World War (Nicholson, 1967; Prest & Stark, 1967) and no significant general trend towards greater income equality in the USA over as long a period as 1910 to 1959 (Kolko, 1962). Equally, the share of company trading profits after taxation in the national incomes of both countries has remained remarkably constant through most of this century apart from the depression period in the USA and periods of war in the UK (Blackburn, 1965; Baran & Sweezy, 1966). Thus businessmen have been able to offset the effects of long-term increases in company taxation rates. Fairly recently there may even have been a widening gap between the lowest and other income levels in the USA (Myrdal, 1963), although in the UK there seems to have been some redistribution of shares away from profits and towards wages since 1964 (Dept. of Employment and Productivity 1968). In contrast to the American situation, in the USSR where income distribution policy is centralized and the individual enterprise plays little part, a previously high inequality of income distribution has been reduced since the later 1950s, chiefly by raising the wages of lower paid employees (Nove, 1968a, 1969).

Income distribution is a major foundation for social stratification and there are some who therefore view the role of the business enterprise in maintaining marked differentials as constituting a major social problem in capitalist society (e.g. Blackburn, 1965).[14] Others would extend managerial responsibility beyond the 'equitable' distribution of income to encompass also the establishment of procedures whereby the

[14] As well as income differentials, variations in fringe benefits and security of tenure also contribute to economic stratification in society. Most concern has been felt for the wage earner in this respect, but some commentators are now also complaining that the managements of large enterprises do not always pay sufficient regard to the economic interests of small shareholders (e.g. *The Times*, 27/7/1968).

surplus available for distribution is also raised. Flanders (1966) has argued that it is one of management's 'internal social responsibilities' to utilize productivity bargaining to this end. Moreover, modern social thinking, in Britain at least, places obligations upon management to compensate adequately before depriving an employee of the right to draw income (cf. the Redundancy Payments Act 1965) and also to locate enterprises where they can provide incomes for persons previously unemployed.

B *Consumption*

The extent to which the modern large business enterprise is able to manipulate consumer behaviour provides a further contentious issue of wide social concern. The possibility that the wants and choices of consumers may be considerably influenced by marketing techniques alarms the liberal as well as the economist who still holds to his traditional view that the 'consumer is (and ought to be) king'. There is also a feeling that business in a relatively unplanned capitalist economy fails to respect socially desirable priorities in its marketing policies, but instead promotes waste through encouraging the conspicuous consumption of goods, into which a short durability has deliberately been designed, by means of extravagant advertising expenditure. This second line of censure can be traced from Veblen's *Theory of the Leisure Class* (1899) to recent critiques such as Baran and Sweezy (1966, Chapter 5) and Packard's journalistic *Waste Makers* (1961).

Galbraith's thesis (1967) on the role of large corporations in modern capitalist economy provides a view of market control that has attracted wide attention. The managements of such enterprises, he argues, have devised ways of manipulating consumer demand for their products. Given the complexities, costs and rigidities of modern industrial investment, it has become necessary for large enterprises not only to design products well in advance of their sale, but to plan their production levels, secure appropriate resources, and set the prices at which they will be sold, also in advance. Hence, there is pressure to mould consumers' preferences so as to ensure fulfilment of these plans. By means of advertising and other selling techniques, Galbraith asserts that, in the main, managements can succeed in this endeavour. In comparison with orthodox economic theory which assumes production to follow the statement of consumer preferences, Galbraith terms this planned procedure the 'revised sequence' in which managements decide on the nature of production and then persuade consumers to purchase their products. This argument has gained the approval of advertising men (such as Kershaw, 1968), but other economists such as Allen (1967) and Meade (1968) believe that it greatly understates the influence of consumer demand partly because Galbraith overlooks the still considerable economic role of small enterprises even in the United States. Moreover, evidence on the effects of advertising suggests that this may only be successful under certain conditions which include an already favourable trend of product demand (cf. Borden, 1942; Telser, 1965; Economists Advisory Group, 1967; Firestone, 1967).[15]

The criticisms which have been levelled at business enterprises in respect of consumer interests have, in effect, concerned aberrations from the free workings of a competitive market system in which theoretically consumer sovereignty is supreme. It is interesting in this connection to note that problems of reconciling business behaviour to consumer interests have been particularly acute in socialist societies where the market mechanism has in the past been most completely discarded. Individual consumer preferences have been disregarded in favour of centrally determined economic planning. Yet even when consumption requirements have been specified in the context of national socio-economic planning, the system of controls and incentives applied to the industrial enterprise has frequently resulted in products of inferior quality or of unsuitable specification; and which are not delivered to schedule (Richman, 1965, Chapter 8). Because of such problems, which obviously affect consumer interests, there are moves to improve resource allocation by incorporating certain elements of the market mechanism into these

[15] The manipulative power of business leaders over other members of society through the use of techniques such as advertising, public relations, and human relations is also exaggerated by critics of 'neocapitalism' such as Marcuse (1964). In broad outline Galbraith and Marcuse present remarkably similar analyses of modern capitalist industrial society. However, the former is a conservative in that he does not see the possibility of an extensive reformulation of prevailing conditions, while Marcuse is a radical in that he does.

planned economies (Miller, 1965; Richman, 1965; Birman, 1968; Nove, 1968a, 1968b).

C *Leisure*

There are several ways in which the business enterprise may influence the quality of leisure available to members of society. In the first place, the quality of a person's experience at work may be linked to the quality of his leisure. Parker (in Parker *et al.*, 1968, Chapter 14) has suggested, in the light of his own and other research, that there may be three patterns of relationship between people's work and their leisure. The first is an *extension pattern* which consists of having leisure activities which are frequently similar in content to work activities, with no sharp distinction being made between the two spheres. This pattern seems to be associated with occupations such as the higher professions, successful businessmen, and some craft work, where the work allows for high intrinsic satisfactions and personal involvement. Second, is a completely contrasting *opposition* pattern which seems to be exhibited by unskilled manual workers, at least some routine clerical workers, and those in arduous and dangerous occupations such as mining and distant-water fishing. Third, Parker distinguishes a *neutrality* pattern falling between the first two, where leisure activities are somewhat differentiated from work, where work is only moderately fulfilling and where satisfaction is found primarily in extrinsic factors. Leisure here functions chiefly as relaxation, while in the opposition pattern it functions mainly as a recuperation from work. Occupations associated with the neutrality pattern include most clerical workers, semi-skilled manual workers and many minor professional employees. Neuloh (1966) classifies the various theoretical interpretations of the relation between work and leisure in a manner comparable to Parker's scheme. Parker concludes after a review of available research that 'the problems of leisure are not likely to be successfully tackled without some consideration of the quality and meaning of working life' (1968, p. 165), and in the present context this clearly posits leisure as a social problem of modern business enterprise.[16]

[16] See also the analyses of this problem presented by Wilensky, 1960; the contributors to Smigel, 1963; and Dumazedier, 1964.

Secondly, the demands made by 'the company' upon its employees' leisure time may constitute a social problem. A study of American trade union leaders, managers on management courses, university students, and managers in enterprises found that there was reasonable agreement as to the spheres in which company influence was legitimate. It was not generally felt that company influence was legitimate in non-work spheres such as family relationships, location of residence, political or religious views, while there was some disagreement about non-company political activities (Schein & Ott, 1962). However, one corollary of the managerialist view that the controllers of business enterprises should manifest their sense of social responsibility in community and public service is, of course, that pressures are likely to be placed on managers to devote some of what is nominally their leisure time to such activities. Whyte (1956) in his *Organization Man* expressed particular concern that managers and white-collar employees were increasingly having to sacrifice family life and leisure for their employing organizations. Other American studies do suggest that the business enterprise can impinge quite substantially upon managerial leisure time (Warner & Abegglen, 1955; Elliott, 1960; Long, 1959). Not much British evidence is available on this issue. However, Burns (1964b) studied 94 managers in 10 companies and found that their average commitment to work was only $43\frac{1}{2}$ hours per week even though this included homework, business lunches, reading and travel for the enterprise.

Finally, Galbraith has argued on several occasions (1958; 1967) that the modern business system, particularly in the United States, has influenced societal values in favour of emphasizing the importance of material possessions and at the cost of aesthetic and social considerations such as the quality of products and their real contribution to human welfare, or the congestion, pollution, noise and despoilment which accompanies their manufacture. In this culture people are encouraged, by means such as business advertising, to own more gadgets rather than to possess more and better leisure. The importance of this problem, though not necessarily Galbraith's own analysis of it, has been widely accepted by social scientists (cf. Kates and Wohlwill, 1966), an acceptance which in Britain has encouraged measures to preserve amenities against the depredations of business enterprises.

5 DISCUSSION

If the humanitarian and the sociological importance of the issues covered by this chapter is now apparent, so also will be the quite substantial gaps in our present knowledge about people's quality of experience at work and outside work. Regarding the former problem, that of quality of experience within the business enterprise, we are now in a good position to identify particular determinants but we know extremely little about their *relative* influence in given situations or about the processes through which their influence is exerted. In terms of the model presented in Figure 1, we need to undertake research which will relate to all the items and processes depicted (rather than taking one or two in isolation) and which will systematically compare carefully selected organizational situations.

The point of moving towards research of this kind is that it should place us in the best position to throw more light on the rival modes of explanation for work attitudes and behaviour which are currently being offered in sociology. We have already come across these different theoretical approaches when discussing the relations between business and environment. The first argues that the economic and technical context sets limits on, and presents 'implications' for, the type of structure and behaviour which will be found at different levels of industrial analysis, right down to individual work roles and the behaviour of their incumbents. The 'needs of the system', as it were, are seen to play a major role in shaping conditions at work. The other approach, that of 'social action' theory, stresses that industrial attitudes, behaviour and organization are simply the products of people's choices and as such must be explained by reference to the social bases for those choices. In other words, we should not think in terms of the 'needs of the system' but rather of the 'needs of those who designed the system and who operate it'. We suggested in Chapter II that the social action perspective does usefully point to certain oversimplifications in the first approach. Nonetheless, there is still every reason to investigate the limits which may be imposed upon social action by the economic, technical and organizational arrangements which *happen to operate* at any given time, and to assess the consequences for the quality of people's work experience.

A great deal of further research is also required into the relationships between work conditions and the quality of people's non-work life. The issue of work in relation to mental health is particularly important. Under conditions where a work environment that satisfies only a limited range of human needs is accepted as part of a 'psychological work contract', are non-work opportunities sufficient to satisfy other needs? More research is required into the whole question of human needs and wants. How are needs related and how far are people's wants substitutable? To what extent are these wants socially defined rather than innately determined? The dangers of business exploitation are now reasonably well recognized so far as they are manifested in economic terms; what now requires attention are the possible socio-psychological costs of business operations and the extent to which these are 'hidden' within family and other private roles.

However, it is apparent from our brief review of some relevant studies that the quality of people's experience within the modern business enterprise is not solely in the hands of those who have the power to shape the form of that enterprise. Apart from the possible economic limits to organizational design, there is also the problem that persons coming from varied social backgrounds and holding different expectations of the work situation present business with correspondingly varied requirements. Nevertheless, it seems likely that far more could be done, even on the basis of our present limited knowledge, to design business organization so as to satisfy further the majority of its employees without any appreciable detriment to economic performance. This possibility forms the main subject of discussion in the following chapter.[17]

---

[17] We do not have the opportunity in this book to discuss the complementary issue of how employees may be better selected to suit organizational conditions, which may to some extent be fixed by the environing characteristics of a particular industry.

CHAPTER V

Conflicting Criteria of Business Performance

The interaction of a business enterprise with its environment leads not only to the immediate economic consequences which comprise the study of market behaviour, but also to the social problems which were the subject of our previous chapter. Today, in most modern industrial societies the economic effectiveness of business enterprise is scrutinized as perhaps never before, but this is also accompanied by a far keener attention to the social consequences of business operations than was previously the rule. Business performance is therefore judged by reference to both economic and social criteria. This chapter begins with a brief examination of these criteria, and then discusses the extent to which they may conflict with respect to the question of employees' quality of experience and general welfare at work.

1 ECONOMIC PERFORMANCE CRITERIA

A privately-owned business enterprise cannot normally survive if it fails to return a financial profit sufficient to meet its liabilities. Indeed, it is quite likely that an enterprise with shares on an open market which made a poor financial return would be drastically reconstituted by means of a take-over at a point before it reached bankruptcy. For this reason alone economic performance criteria must remain paramount for those in control of a private enterprise. This implies in turn that the attention which these businessmen can give to social objectives is subject to economic limits. The important question sociologically is how wide and how flexible are these limits?

Publicly owned business enterprise may have available to

finance its losses the much more extensive reserves of the public purse. In fact, such enterprise may be enjoined as a matter of policy to follow certain socially desirable objectives even when, as with slowing the rate of redundancies, these are at the expense of maximum economic return. Richman (1965, p. 19) estimated that 20% of all Soviet enterprises were operating at a planned loss. The early years of nationalized industry in Britain were accompanied by considerable debate among politicians, and confusion among managements, as to the balance which should be struck between the possible economic and social objectives open to such enterprises. Nevertheless, in more recent years the balance has swung towards an emphasis on clearer economic performance criteria, both in the case of British nationalized industry with the laying down of target rates of return (Cmnd. 1337, 1961; Tivey, 1966; Cmnd. 3437, 1967), and of Soviet industry with the move towards fewer planning indicators in which profits are given a substantially increased role (Birman, 1968; Nove, 1968a).

We cannot in the present context discuss economic performance indicators in any detail.[1] A great many are available and serve different purposes, though in some cases they vary only in relatively minor points of definition (as with various measures of profit earned). A choice is available at the conceptual level between, for example, (i) *productivity* which refers to an input-output balance often measured in terms of physical production rather than value of disposable products; (ii) *profitability* which refers to the overall financial success of an enterprise over a delimited period of time; and (iii) *effectiveness* which refers to the overall success of an enterprise both over a recent period and also with respect to provision for future success (this third concept is sometimes extended to embrace non-economic performance as well). Two primary economic indicators are profit in relation to the value of net resources owned by the enterprise, and rate of growth particularly of assets and of sales. Taken together these two indicators give a reasonable assessment of an enterprise's economic effectiveness. Global indicators such as these two subsume other subsidiary indices such as various cost

[1] For further reference on economic performance criteria see Lewis, 1955; Ingham & Harrington, 1958; Wasserman, 1959; Lomax, 1965.

ratios, while they also indicate the overall level of enterprise achievement from which rewards to sectional interests derive.

An important problem in the analysis of enterprise performance lies in the choice between what Etzioni has called a 'goal-model' and a 'system-model' of organizational effectiveness (Etzioni, 1960; cf. Yuchtman & Seashore, 1967). That is, the choice between assessing performance by the extent to which specified goals have been achieved, and assessing it by comparison with a theoretically optimum distribution of resources among various organizational requirements. This latter, the system-model, allows not only for the presence of officially stated goals, but for the presence of other goals which may also be held in respect of organizational functioning. It thus provides a perspective that is appropriate for the consideration of social as well as economic objectives.

2 SOCIAL PERFORMANCE CRITERIA

Classical economic theory posited that under certain limiting assumptions, such as perfect competition and consumer 'sovereignty' in the marketplace, profit maximizing behaviour by the businessman would itself promote the maximum possible social welfare[2] (cf. Lectures on Economic Science, 1870; Kreps, 1962). This view is discredited today with the knowledge that market imperfections can operate to the consumer's expense, and that business operations can give rise to social costs which affect parties outside the immediate market relationships of an enterprise. In fact, a growing appreciation of how the market mechanism may be unable to control business activities for the wider social benefit has been one of the main reasons for the concern over business power in modern industrial society which we found, in Chapter III, to be so evident.

Sociologists and social commentators have for some time been concerned that business was failing to meet what they regarded as essential social criteria. Marx argued that capitalist industry necessarily failed to satisfy any acceptable social criteria, an observation which was largely true of the time

[2] We recognize, but cannot discuss in this short review, the question of conflicting value judgements which is begged by the use of terms such as 'welfare' or 'utility'. For a thoughtful analysis of this problem in the context of welfare economics see Little (1957, Chapter V).

when he wrote (Bottomore & Rubel, 1956). Veblen felt that man's true fulfilment through the pursuit of workmanship was endangered by the growth of 'parasitic' occupations such as banking and marketing which accompanied the development of the capitalist economic system. He associated these new occupations with the wasteful production of goods valued more as a means for conspicuous consumption by wealthy social parasites than because of their intrinsic worth (Riesman, 1953). Veblen was thus concerned with a threat to 'meaningful' work and to consumer welfare in terms of securing value for money. Tawney (1921) also attacked the sickness of the acquisitive society which he felt characterized Britain and other 'modern societies'. Wealth which had accrued to 'functionless property'—to absentee ownership—was squandered by that small section of society while others went in need. Private self-interest was encouraged at the expense of public duty. In particular, Tawney argued that the solution to this social disease lay with industry. This had to be restructured so that authority rested not on ownership but on function; and this would be authority directly responsible to those whose quality of life was affected by industry—to employees and consumers in particular.

There have been many other commentators who were pioneers in positing social criteria for business performance. One may instance Robert Owen who both advocated and introduced improved working conditions, shortened working hours, and allowed for appeal against managerial actions in his factories (Urwick & Brech, 1947). Equally, the Webbs deserve mention with their determination to promote industrial democracy (S. & B. Webb, 1897). And Pope Leo XIII whose encyclical *Rerum Novarum* (1891) called for a wider distribution of property ownership, minimum wage legislation, and state intervention in business to protect those in need.

It is possible to classify many of the demands of these pioneering thinkers, together with more recent views, into the following areas of social concern:

A *Quality of experience at work*
Relevant criteria of performance include:

(i) work should not possess deleterious physical, psychological or social consequences for employees;

(ii) work should possess the maximum possible opportunities to satisfy employee expectations and wants;
(iii) there should be opportunities for personal advancement within the employing organization.

B *The means of livelihood,* including:
(i) adequate levels of income should be provided for moderate hours of work and personal effort;
(ii) there should be security of employment and the financial means to achieve changes of employment when these are necessary.

C *Regard for consumer and community welfare,* including:
(i) lack of consumer exploitation for excess profits;
(ii) measures to keep unaesthetic consequences of business operations to the minimum.

D *Reduction of inequalities,* including:
(i) attempts to reduce differentials of income, privileges, and status;
(ii) the equal representation of different interests and views in business decision-making.

Government legislation and trade union action have in most industrial societies gone some way towards ensuring that those in control of business enterprises meet these social criteria, particularly by establishing minimum standards with respect to categories A–C. However, there are still many today who feel that business does not as a rule do enough to assist the reduction of inequalities in society. One concept which is frequently mentioned, both as a progression towards reduced inequality within enterprises and as a means to secure other socially valued objectives, is that of 'participation' in decision-making. The idea of participation has in fact secured sufficient popular and academic attention to warrant some examination at this point.

Participation conveys quite different meanings to commentators representing diverse political standpoints. In the main, those who advocate forms of participation which embrace both the determination of business goals as well as the establishment of means to achieve the goals represent a left-wing non-managerial viewpoint. Those who restrict the scope of participation merely to the determination of means, with the goals already determined by management, tend to have another and distinctly managerial objective. Moreover, the proposed structures of participation also vary. One alternative lays most emphasis on a relatively formal organization-wide system of representation, exemplified by the works council. Another stresses informal small group decision-making, which is oriented more towards a continuous rather than intermittent review of problems. Lammers (1967) has labelled these two structures 'indirect' and 'direct' participation. It is possible to represent the four basic types of participation which result by means of a diagram:[3]

FIGURE 2—Forms of Participation

SCOPE OF DECISION-MAKING

	GOALS+MEANS ('DEMOCRATIC')	MEANS ONLY ('CONSERVATIVE')
WHOLE ORGANIZATION	A	B
SMALL- GROUP	D	C

FOCAL LEVEL

Type A participation is the goal of many British left-wing intellectuals and of some trade union leaders. The Yugoslav experiment in workers' control represents the best-known contemporary example of this type. Some British advocates derive encouragement from Yugoslav experience (e.g. Singleton & Topham, 1963), while others are more cautious (e.g. Coates, 1965). Another system of participation which falls into category A is 'productivity bargaining' when this involves a joint reconsideration of business policies (Flanders, 1964). The works council in operation at Renold Chains Ltd since the First World War, and at the Glacier Metal Com-

[3] Although these four types are represented separately for purposes of analysis one might find hybrid arrangements in actual practice. The above classification is, of course, a simplified one. Blumberg, for instance, identifies ten stages between a fully democratic and a purely nominal form of participation with respect to the scope of decision-making involved (1968, p. 71).

pany since 1949, also came close to type A, at least in their formal provisions (Renold, 1950; Brown, 1960). The Labour Party's proposals for increased employee rights of access to company information, and for the extension of collective bargaining to cover all aspects of management, again represent a type A approach (*The Times* 29/7/1968). Writers such as Sturmthal (1964) and Das (1964) have provided useful reviews of the provision for this type of participation to be found in a number of industrial societies.

Type D participation is less frequently advocated, a problem being that it is somewhat removed organizationally from the level at which major policy decisions are normally taken. This type is associated with the idea of the 'self-governing work group'. As such it represents freedom *from* certain management controls rather than an extensive share *in* management decision-making. This idea was advocated by Gillespie (1948) and more recently by Clegg (1960); up to a point it operated at the Standard Motor Company for a few years before 1956 (Melman, 1958). This form of participation has also been attempted in some small companies where indeed the work group may approximate to the whole work force, and hence where type D tends to merge into type A (Bond-Williams, 1953).

The advocates of types A and D participation are motivated by the belief that the quality of business' social performance can effectively be raised by broadening the base upon which business policy rests—especially with respect to issues such as the quality of work experience, income distribution or security of tenure. In contrast, the advocates of types B and C participation are limited in their proposals by a concern that business social performance should not be at the expense of the effective managerial authority they claim to be necessary for economic success. In effect, these types of participation aim to 'conserve' managerial prerogatives. Type B approximates to the now traditional model of joint consultation (cf. Walpole, 1944) which has today been widely accepted as a disappointment (Clegg, 1960). Drucker's proposals for establishing 'self-governing plant communities' also falls into category B, although his frame of reference is wider than that typical of joint consultation (1943, 1946, 1951). For instance, he argues that the achievement of conditions favourable to employee participation will depend on suitable modifications to plant technology, and on giving employees greater discretion and more company information (Drucker, 1946, Chapter III).

Type C participation derives largely from the human relations approach associated particularly with Mayo (1945) and Whitehead (1936), and from the 'group dynamics' school of Lewin and his students (cf. Cartwright & Zander, 1960). Many advocates of this type lay greatest stress on its potential as a managerial technique to facilitate the acceptance of change by employees (e.g. Coch & French, 1948; McGregor, 1960; Likert, 1961, 1967; Marrow, *et al.*, 1967). Argyris (1957, 1960, 1964) is perhaps the best known writer who retains a broader interest in type C participation as a means to alleviate a social problem created by business (organizational limits on personal self-actualization), in addition to its possibilities for creating harmony with managerial goals.

A concept such as employee participation in one form attracts support from those who see industrial democracy as a socially desirable objective and as a means to securing other social objectives; in another form participation gains adherents who view it as a managerial technique which will enhance the economic performance of a business enterprise. It is in this context that recent surveys of the participation literature by Lammers (1967) and Blumberg (1968) are especially thought provoking. For these writers conclude that an extension of participative arrangements in industry offers a major opportunity both for enhancing economic performance and for mitigating the alienating conditions found in so many contemporary work environments. Lammers concludes that we should not adopt a 'zero-sum' view of power in organizations, but rather we should recognize that an increase in the power of lower-level employees is not necessarily at the expense of the power held by managerial personnel. Increased participation in decision-making can, as Lammers illustrates, lead to improved economic effectiveness by improving the information on which business decisions are based and by increasing the acceptability of those decisions throughout an enterprise. Blumberg marshals a great amount of evidence to support the view that moves towards industrial democracy are more likely to provide an effective response to the problem of reconciling economic and social criteria of business performance than the other solutions which have been advanced, such as seeking compensation for work alienation in leisure activities, in the advance of automation, in job enlargement, or even in a rejection of industrialism itself.

The debate about participation thus reflects the central issue with which this chapter is concerned, namely, 'in what form and to what extent are social objectives compatible with the economic objectives of business?' This is an issue of immense sociological importance, but of formidable complexity, which social scientists have so far scarcely begun to answer. During the remainder of this chapter we shall explore certain aspects of the problem, focusing on the extent to which it may be possible to design organizational arrangements that are conducive to the economic effectiveness of a business enterprise, yet also enhance the well-being experienced by its employees. We have in mind here the ways in which people's jobs and immediate working environments are structured by administrative mechanisms, technology and so on. It seems likely that these factors have at least as great an influence on people's work experiences as does the opportunity to participate in decision-making, especially if the latter only takes an 'indirect' form.

3 ECONOMIC EFFECTIVENESS AND EMPLOYEE WELFARE

The nature of the available sociological evidence forces us, as in the previous chapter, to rely heavily upon job satisfaction as an indicator of employee welfare.[4] We shall therefore be primarily concerned with an assessment of how far high employee satisfaction appears to be compatible with a high

---

[4] Apparently more objective criteria such as levels of financial reward are not necessarily adequate indicators of the welfare *experienced* by employees. For example, if one accepts psychological equity theory, it is not possible to conclude that an increase in an employee's income necessarily raises his overall level of welfare. Quite apart from the possibility that the extra income may be at the cost of other benefits, if the employee happens to believe that he does not deserve the extra income he may suffer discomforting guilt feelings which *for him* could more than offset any benefits which the additional money can buy (cf. Jaques, 1961; Vroom, 1964, pp. 167–72).

economic effectiveness of business enterprises. There are four questions which are relevant to this assessment:

(i) Which organizational characteristics of business enterprise are conducive to employee welfare?

(ii) Is high employee welfare associated with high individual contributions to the economic effectiveness of an enterprise?

(iii) Are the organizational characteristics conducive to employee welfare themselves compatible with high overall economic effectiveness of an enterprise?

(iv) In the light of answers to the previous questions, what managerial policies seem best suited to inducing high economic effectiveness of an enterprise while at the same time enhancing its contribution to employee welfare?

(i) In chapter IV we concluded that the degree of satisfaction which people felt at work depended upon their own work identity in relation to the organizational characteristics of their workplace. These organizational characteristics can therefore possess some independent influence on the level of welfare experienced by employees, and we identified certain structural and technological features which in an extreme form would almost certainly result in lower job satisfaction whatever employees' prior expectations. Such features included a high specialization, routinization and repetitiveness of tasks, low job autonomy, and the absence of socially compact and cohesive working groups. Certain of the structural features were found to be associated with large organizational size.

Apart from size and technology, there is a further organizational characteristic which may encourage a low sense of employee welfare. There is already some evidence that rapid organizational change, particularly in the nature of work performed,[5] may lead to a greater sense of personal insecurity and job dissatisfaction than would otherwise be the case (Burns & Stalker, 1961; Hage & Aiken, 1968). Apart from the problems of conflict and co-ordination which rapid change brings (Lawrence & Lorsch, 1967), people in these situations appear often to experience personal insecurity (especially

[5] This is the 'programme change' conceptualized by Hage and Aiken (1967).

Burns & Stalker, 1961). The management of change to optimize both economic effectiveness and employee welfare is a subject requiring much further research.

(ii) It was a fundamental tenet of human relations theory that high employee welfare manifested in high 'morale' (generalized job satisfaction) would motivate them to make a maximum contribution towards productivity. In this posited relationship lay the hope of a business system capable of meeting both society's economic and social needs (Whitehead, 1936; Mayo, 1945).

In the event, it has become clear that there is no straight-forward relationship between the two variables. After reviewing most of the extensive available research, Vroom (1964) concluded that 'Correlations between these variables vary within an extremely large range and the median correlation of ·14 has little theoretical or practical importance' (p. 186). Vroom pointed out that there is good reason to believe that the determinants of job satisfaction and of job performance are not identical, and more particularly that there is no necessary relationship between valued rewards and job performance: 'Individuals are satisfied with their jobs to the extent which their jobs provide them with what they desire, and they perform effectively in them to the extent that effective performance leads to the attainment of what they desire' (1964, p. 264). A belief of employees that effective performance as defined by management may place their longer-term welfare at risk is evident in cases where they adopt measures to limit their levels of output (cf. Roethlisberger & Dickson, 1939; Collins, Dalton & Roy, 1946; Roy, 1952; Hickson, 1961; Lupton, 1963). Alternatively, Goode and Fowler (1949) describe a case where tough managerial policies towards employees who mostly possessed poor employment alternatives induced high effort along with low morale.

However, certain qualifications must be made to this analysis. The fact that low job satisfaction is consistently associated with high levels of labour turnover, and is quite frequently associated with high levels of absenteeism (Vroom, 1964, p. 186), does suggest that it is not enough to measure job performance without costing turnover and absence as well. It seems to have been the general rule not to have done this, and to this extent Vroom's median correlation of .14 is probably too low. Secondly, Likert (1961) makes the point that a situation in which low job satisfaction is associated with high employee performance (e.g. Morse & Reimer, 1956) may not persist over the long-run, because (for one reason) employees will leave their jobs as soon as alternatives are available which give them a superior contributions-inducements balance (March & Simon, 1958). Thirdly, in assessments of job performance quality of work should be given an appropriate economic value alongside quantity. Therefore, before we can be sure about the relationship of job satisfaction with job performance, we will require both more sophisticated assessments of job performance and further exploration of the conditions affecting the different strengths of relationship that have been found.

(iii) There appears on present evidence to be no necessary relationship between job satisfaction and individual contributions to the economic effectiveness of an enterprise. However, if we move to the level of a whole enterprise or of an organizational unit, is it the case that factors conducive to higher job satisfaction (especially the avoidance of large size, of certain technological features, and of rapid change), are themselves compatible with maximum economic effectiveness? And if an enterprise should happen to possess an economically optimum size, technology and rate of innovation, what freedom is there left to vary structural attributes within these limits in order to enhance employee welfare? We consider these questions in turn.

A *Size, technology, change and economic effectiveness*
Economists have long debated the necessity of large scale for maximum economic effectiveness (Robinson, 1953; Penrose, 1959). Large *plant* size, some argue, may be necessary to reap technological economies of scale if long-run unit costs of production fall with increases of output. Large *company* size may bring other economic advantages such as (i) the ability to underwrite the risks associated with research and development (cf. Schumpeter, 1942; Galbraith, 1952; Blackett, 1968); (ii) enhanced bargaining power in the company's markets including the ability to attract finance on better terms because of its apparently greater security;[6] and (iii) economies in

[6] Enhanced market bargaining powers resulting from large size do

marketing and distribution. What evidence is there to support these propositions?

The assessment of technological scale economies has been hampered by substantial methodological problems. Recently Pratten and Dean (1965) have investigated the extent of such economies of scale in four British industries (book printing, footwear manufacture, steel production and oil refining). They concluded that technological economies of scale do exist in these industries, particularly the last two. Similar conclusions have been reached in respect of other industries—for instance, vehicles (Maxcy & Silberston, 1959) and retailing (McClelland, 1966)—as well as over a range of British and German plants (Ray, 1966) and over a selection of Indian industries (Mukerji, 1963). However, such results only indicate the presence of scale economies in plants or shops. It is quite possible to have large companies operating a large number of small plants which are not benefiting greatly from technological economies of scale. Thus in 1958, Britain's eight largest companies were running no less than 467 separate establishments (the *Economist*, 1967), even though in the years previous to 1958 there had in most industries been a movement towards operating fewer and larger plants (Armstrong & Silberston, 1965).

Some, mainly American, evidence is available on the Research and Development advantages which large company size may offer. Comparing firms of all sizes, company size appears as a very important determinant of company R & D expenditure (F.B.I., 1961; Freeman, 1962; Hamberg, 1964; the *Economist*, 1967). However, larger firms in some industries may spend less on R & D as a proportion of their sales than smaller ones (Mansfield, 1964b; Scherer, 1965) or employ a lower percentage of their total personnel on R & D (Hamberg, 1964)—though this could be interpreted as indicating some economies in larger R & D expenditures. It also appears that larger firms may in some industries account for a relatively large share of innovation—the product of R & D (Mansfield, 1963a), and be quicker to

---

not necessarily encourage an efficient use of economic resources by an enterprise. These powers may be misused, creating a divergence between private and public economic performance. This problem of monopolistic or oligopolistic power has been touched upon in Chapters III and IV.

adopt new techniques when they become available (Mansfield, 1963b).

Finally, turning to the overall economic performance of business enterprises it appears that while larger enterprises generally succeed in securing a more stable pattern of performance over time, they do not either in the United Kingdom or the United States secure a superior level of profitability (Ferguson, 1960; Barron, 1967; Samuels & Smyth, 1968). Indeed, the last two studies (which were independent studies of medium to very large UK firms) both showed an inverse relationship between company size and level of profit to assets.[7]

To summarize, the available evidence on size of business enterprise and economic effectiveness is far from clear. Some recent investigation suggests that the economic advantages of bigness may have been exaggerated in the past. In this respect, a great deal depends on whether large company size is matched by large plant size affording technological scale economies. There is also good reason to believe that particular industry characteristics can affect this issue (cf. Barron, 1967). For instance, the rate of change and uncertainty experienced may seriously limit size advantages (Schwartzman, 1963), as might restricted product market sizes and also the organizational problems which we suggested earlier could arise with large scale.

Florence (1962) found that there was an association between large plant size and greater capital intensity, which may serve as some indication of macro-technological integration.[8] If technological economies of scale are present, and if a shift to larger outputs of standardized products contributes to these economies through allowing more rationalized and integrated production processes, then one may suggest that in some circumstances particular technologies will be more effective economically than others. This would seem to apply to a move from small to large batch production if the nature of the product and its market demand allows. It is more difficult to establish the relationship between technology and

[7] These results should be regarded as tentative since they may have been distorted by certain methodological problems, particularly the greater frequency with which larger companies appear to revalue their assets upwards.

[8] Unpublished results of research by the Industrial Administration Research Unit at the University of Aston lend some support to the size/technology association for manufacturing organizations.

economic effectiveness than is the case with size, since so much depends on factors such as the technical nature of the product and the state of knowledge relevant to its production. However, some economic limits will undoubtedly operate on the production technology which can be employed by a particular business enterprise.

Finally, the nature of its market and technical environment may oblige an enterprise to maintain a high rate of change in its work programmes. If market competition is keen and based more on product substitution (deriving from innovation) than on low price (deriving from low costs), as is generally true of the pharmaceuticals industry (Cooper, 1966), then a firm wishing to remain economically effective will face pressures to introduce new products relatively frequently. The possible relationships of change with size and technology require further investigation. Robinson (1953) has suggested that the need for adaptability sets large size and highly integrated technology at a disadvantage, other things being equal.[9]

B *Organizational choice*

While there may be limits within which size, technology and rate of change should fall if an enterprise wishes to optimize its economic performance, these limits do not seem capable of very precise definition as yet. This fact alone should make us wary of the economic determinism which lurks, for instance, in Galbraith's recent work (1967). In addition, one can find evidence suggesting that there are opportunities for designing into an organizational structure features which enhance job satisfaction and other aspects of employee welfare without apparent detriment to economic effectiveness.

The work of the Tavistock Institute of Human Relations, centring on the concept of a *'socio-technical system'*, has greatly increased our appreciation that alternative forms of work organization are possible within a given set of technological limits. This concept posits both the independent

---

[9] Other things may not, of course, be equal. Thus a larger firm may be able to employ extra specialists whose job it is to give early warning of changing external conditions, which might offset some of the rigidities of organization structure associated with scale. Nor would there appear to be any necessary association between rates of product change and the macro-technology employed—see Chapter VI below.

values and interdependency of the technological, social and economic dimensions of work (Emery, 1959; Emery & Trist, 1960). An application of this concept indicates that while the technology of an enterprise sets limits to the type of workplace social organization which is possible, this social organization has properties of its own which can be analysed and manipulated within the technological limits. Both technology and social organization are themselves limited by the need to maintain the economic viability of the enterprise.

The socio-technical system approach has been applied successfully in British coalmines and Indian textile mills by teams under Trist (Trist & Bamforth, 1951; Trist *et al.*, 1963) and Rice respectively (Rice, 1958, 1963). In each case, within given technological situations, it was possible to break away from the existing assumptions that lay behind work organization, and to design new structures which not only enhanced job satisfaction but also improved job performance. In a more recent series of investigations exploring a different set of socio-technical systems—including marketing, dry cleaning and an airline—somewhat less scope was found for restructuring work organization to give both greater satisfaction and job performance (Miller & Rice, 1967). One problem here was that the work situations were in some cases ones which had to remain adaptable to change, and the restructuring of a work organization to afford greater satisfaction to employees was liable to induce them to resist further change in order to preserve their newly-enhanced welfare. Melman's study (1958) of the Standard Motor Company also illustrates the possibilities of designing alternative structural arrangements within a given technological situation.

There would seem to be widespread opportunities for socio-technical engineering, since other recent research has indicated that (*pace* Woodward, 1958, 1965) many features of organizational structure need not be governed closely by the technology employed (Hickson *et al.*, 1969). However, the conditions determining the success of this approach still require further study. We have already stressed, for instance, that one such condition lies in the work identity held by the employees concerned, a point which Hulin and Blood's review of job enlargement experiments brings home forcefully (1968).

There is possibly less organizational choice within the limits set by size. Certainly, available research has shown much less variation of organizational structures at given size levels than with given technologies (Pugh *et al.*, 1969).[10] A more restricted degree of organizational choice may explain why Porter and Lawler's review of research (1965) concluded that 'sub-unit size' was strongly related to job satisfaction and its behavioural indicators—remembering that many of their 'sub-units' were whole plants. Nevertheless, a firm operating in conditions where technological economies of scale were unimportant (perhaps because its market demand changed too much to allow for standardized production) would be able to design its production facilities so as to keep plant size relatively small. And even within a large plant it may prove possible to allocate functions so as to encourage the formation of small and cohesive working groups which, other things being equal, promote greater job satisfaction. There is no obvious reason why such policies should prejudice the economic viability of an enterprise.

Research into the organizational requirements for effectively coping with varying rates of change is as yet too undeveloped for extensive conclusions to be drawn. However, although the most important studies (Burns & Stalker, 1961; Lawrence & Lorsch, 1967; Hage & Aiken, 1968) do agree that certain broad structural features are optimal for coping with change, their detailed conclusions differ which suggests the possibility of some choice. For instance, Lawrence and Lorsch recommend different methods of integrating the work of specialists under conditions of change to those suggested by Burns and Stalker.

(iv) The model of work experience presented in the previous chapter and the perspectives of organizational design just mentioned speak for a multi-variate analysis of attitudes and behaviour within the business enterprise. In turn, this implies that managerial policies which are directed to the modification of single or only few variables do not hold out more than a limited possibility of reconciling economic and social goals. For this reason, the currently popular neo-human relations approach is a limited one. For it proposes a form of

[10] In this research the organizational units whose size was measured were sometimes whole companies and sometimes merely sub-unit establishments.

employee participation which is confined to areas that are managerially defined, and it tends to exclude the determination of many policies which have direct implications for work organization and the welfare of the people employed in it. Thus participation is not extended to matters such as the determination of income differentials, or promotion opportunities, or the choice of first-line supervision (cf. Strauss, 1963a, 1963b; Davies, 1967).

Similarly, many would argue today that the piecemeal approach to labour relations has resulted in chaotic wage agreements, resistance to change, and restrictive working practices. This should give way to a new form of relationship which is based on extensive participation encompassing the determination of all relevant aspects of the work situation. This comprehensive approach is represented in the concept of 'productivity bargaining', though it was foreshadowed by the procedures operating in a few British firms such as Renold Chains and Glacier Metal (Renold, 1950; Brown, 1960). At its best, productivity bargaining not only contributes towards the economic effectiveness of an enterprise, but it also encourages managers and employers to act 'in ways that pay regard to the wider social consequences of their actions' (Flanders, 1966, p. 21). By combining 'conflictual' with 'consensual' participation (Delamotte, 1959), productivity bargaining is in tune with the fundamental characteristics of relationships in industry.[11]

Productivity bargaining is an important variant of employee participation in decision-making within the business enterprise. Considerable disappointment has been expressed with other experiments allowing for employee participation in determining the goals and procedures of the whole enterprise —'Type A' participation—which have taken place in countries such as Israel, Western Germany and Yugoslavia (Clegg, 1960; Derber, 1963; Das, 1964; Kolaja, 1965; Peterson, 1968).[12] In terms of the analysis we have followed, the success or failure of a participative system should in large part be explicable by reference to (i) employees' own expectations

[11] Productivity bargaining is discussed at some length in Alan Fox's contribution to this series.

[12] A recent report suggests that such pessimism is exaggerated so far as Yugoslavia is concerned (Riddell, 1968).

of participation in decision-making, and (ii) the relevance to employees' own work environment of issues covered by the participative system. Available research suggests some cross-cultural differences in (i) (French *et al.*, 1960), and also differences in employee expectations of participation which can be ascribed to the power and intrinsic satisfaction which their work role affords to them, and hence to the involvement which they experience in the enterprise (cf. Bassoul *et al.*, 1960; Banks, 1963b; Holter, 1965). As an instance of point (ii), the widespread failure of 'joint consultation' in Britain and of the 'comités d'entreprise' in France can largely be ascribed to the constitutional inability of such procedures to cope with the issues which employees regard as the most important (Clegg, 1960; Durand, 1962). In general support of this argument, one may suggest that the Tavistock Institute experiments in British coalmines were successful because (i) their new 'composite' work system allowed for closer social interaction which accorded well with the traditionally close relationships of mining communities (Dennis *et al.*, 1957; Sigal, 1960), and because (ii) the change allowed for more employee determination of their immediate work environment.

Productivity bargaining conforms to the traditional expectations of British workers that participation in industry should be effected through elected representatives. In contrast to the narrow scope of joint consultation, productivity bargaining embraces a wide range of interrelated variables of considerable importance to all parties concerned. Productivity bargaining therefore represents a frame of mind sympathetic to the challenge of shaping the underlying organization of business enterprises in ways which will advance equally the objectives of both managements and employees. If it can become a regular and continuous process, productivity bargaining would seem to offer considerable potential as a means for achieving in a complementary manner many of the economic and social objectives which are ascribed to the business enterprise in modern industrial society.

4 DISCUSSION

It would appear Gouldner (1955) was right when he argued that students of organization have been too pessimistic about the possibilities of attaining new structural forms which can enhance the welfare experienced by employees. In this connection, the size of enterprises and their establishments emerges as the most problematic limitation to organizational choice. The increasing pressures of international competition, and the economies of scale apparent in the research activities of our vital and expanding science-based industries, are among the factors which place a premium on large size. Indeed, for reasons such as these, governments in the West are noticeably softening their previous hostility to large size, even to the point of accepting corollaries such as product monopoly (cf. Hacker, 1965a). Few of the once eagerly-discussed reforms to ensure that large enterprises make some effort to maintain employee welfare and to follow other social objectives are received with great enthusiasm any more. For example, public ownership has disappointed those who hoped it would show a lead towards industrial democracy or towards new levels of employee welfare, because publicly-owned enterprises have not been able to avoid economic and bureaucratic limits on these objectives. The most successful organizational design in this respect remains the Yugoslavian, and this, too, has faced considerable problems (Riddell, 1968).

The challenge here to sociologists lies in ascertaining more comprehensively the orientations to work held by different groups in society, and in determining more precisely the economic limits to designing organizational forms to accommodate such orientations. The conditions under which these limits apply must also be established. Relevant research is being undertaken by British sociologists both into work orientations (Brown & Brannen, 1968; Silverman, 1968a) and into the relationship of organization to the effectiveness of enterprises (Child, 1967). Nevertheless, these represent but the very early stages of response to this most important task, which at its broadest is one of finding the means of enhancing both the social and economic performance of the business enterprise.

The conditions in which the business enterprise performs are themselves changing in modern industrial societies. To close our review, we consider the implications of some current changes for the kind of issues with which this book has been concerned.

CHAPTER VI

Emerging Patterns

1 AN AGE OF TECHNICAL PROGRESS

It has become an article of faith in modern industrial societies that ours is an age of technical progress. Technical progress, which may be defined as 'the introduction of important new or improved products or processes' (Maclaurin, 1954), is regarded as the key to sustained economic growth and rising standards of living in the advanced economies of capitalist (Shanks, 1967) and of communist societies (Auerhan, 1966).[1] For the business enterprise, technical progress takes the form of an increasingly complex and dynamic technical environment which may also induce changes in product market expectations and in the characteristics of available factors of production (Emery & Trist, 1965, p. 21).

Technical progress, or 'innovation', is notoriously difficult to measure directly, and less direct indicators such as numbers of patents registered can be misleading (Ames, 1961). However, expenditure on Research and Development, which in the United States has been found to be an extremely good indicator of the number of patents (Mueller, 1966) and of 'significant inventions' (Mansfield, 1964b), serves as some guide to the rate of technical progress. This has been particularly rapid in the United States where R & D expenditure

---

[1] Some dissent from this prevailing view, e.g. Stettner, 1966, pp. 459–60. However, we have chosen to discuss technical progress in this chapter because it represents a contemporary social phenomenon which is to a large extent centred on the business enterprise and which has widespread social consequences. It is, of course, not the only important development within modern industrial societies, but it is a central one. Other sociologists discussing emerging social trends have for this reason also given considerable attention to the subject (cf. Friedmann, 1964 and Faunce, 1968).

rose by over 50% between 1957 and 1964. In 1962 US expenditure on R & D averaged 3·1% of total national income, that in the USSR between $2\frac{1}{2}$% and 3%, in the UK 2·2%, and in western Europe as a whole 1·6% (Shanks, 1967, p. 44). These percentages tend to mask the very large expenditures which are involved (£882·9 million in the UK during the financial year 1966–7), and also the steady rise in these outlays. Thus total UK R & D expenditure rose at an average rate of almost 7% annually over the five years 1961–2 to 1966–7, while R & D in private industry rose at an average rate of almost 9% annually over the same period (Annual Abstract of Statistics, 1968).

The industries primarily affected by this technical progress are relatively few in number, but they assume a disproportionate importance as the most dynamic sectors of modern economies. This is true, above all, of the 'science-based' industries: aircraft production, chemicals, scientific instruments, electronics and a large part of the electrical industry. These industries account for about three-quarters of all R & D expenditure in British industry (Jones, 1965). Such industries are not yet 'typical', but they are becoming more so. Nor is technical progress itself a new phenomenon, but it has been speeding up and is having increasingly important consequences for the nature of business enterprises and for their relationships with other social institutions.

The application of technical progress to a business enterprise takes two main forms. The first is *product innovation,* that is innovation in goods or services produced and in the programmes of work they involve. This innovation represents an important aspect of what Hage and Aiken (1967) call 'programme change'. The second form is *technological innovation,* that is innovation in the techniques applied to production. We shall in this connection restrict our use of the term 'technology' to the equipment used in the workflows of a business enterprise and the interrelationship of the operations to which the equipment is applied (cf. Pugh *et al.,* 1963).[2]

The response of a business enterprise to technical progress

[2] There has been a great deal of unnecessary confusion between the technical make-up of a product and the techniques applied to its production. Most sociologists (and indeed economists) have employed the

may entail new types of relationship with its environment, while the application of technical progress may affect the organization of an enterprise, the quality of experience of its employees, and social welfare more generally. These have been some of the main issues covered in previous chapters, and we now conclude by examining to what extent they may be influenced by current patterns of innovation.

2 TECHNICAL PROGRESS, CHANGE AND BUSINESS ENVIRONMENT

Technical progress tends to encourage a greater degree of interdependence between a business enterprise and its environment for three main reasons. First, it is normally associated with increasing environmental change and complexity, presenting a business enterprise with a growth of more sophisticated information relevant to its various functions. The enterprise is encouraged to employ specialists in differentiated roles in order to cope with this development (Lawrence & Lorsch, 1967). These specialists are likely to have an extensive training and professional involvement. They are employed to permit more effective communication between the enterprise and its environment, communication relevant to the successful operation of functions such as research, production engineering, or technical sales. Greater professional specialization of this kind will not only permit an

---

concept of technology, as we do, to refer to production processes (e.g. Emery & Trist, 1960; Blauner, 1964; Turner & Lawrence, 1965; Woodward, 1965; Brown, 1966; Lave, 1966; Perrow, 1967; Thompson, 1967). However, Harvey (1968) has defined technology in this orthodox way but at the same time confusingly measured it by reference to rates of product change, that is change in product make-up. It is true that a product innovation will usually require some change in micro-technology; at least some minor adjustments in equipment settings or tooling. But there is not necessarily any consistent relationship between product make-up and production technology, or between product innovation and technological innovation. For one thing the economics of the two are distinct. Thus relatively traditional techniques may still represent the most economic way of producing goods whose design is constantly being modified to incorporate highly sophisticated new features. Equally it may become economic to replace a machine by a technically more sophisticated one in the manufacture of a product whose specifications remain the same.

enterprise to take account of environmental change, it will also tend to promote more rapid change within the enterprise (Hage & Aiken, 1967, 1968).

Second, although environmental change puts a premium on enterprise adaptability and therefore on small size—if we follow Robinson (1953), the pursuit and application of technical progress set up pressures towards growing scale. The studies reviewed in Chapter V suggest that R & D may often only be economic once a certain size of enterprise is reached. Thus even where there are few manufacturing economies of scale, as in the pharmaceuticals industry, a larger enterprise will be in a better position to cover R & D costs and to accept the high investment risk which is involved (cf. Dunning, 1965; Cooper, 1966). Similarly the costs of investing in technological innovation, especially advanced automation systems, may cause this to be concentrated in larger enterprises (Stettner, 1966, p. 454), and indeed this is often given as the reason for already large companies to merge (cf. report on the British banks, *The Times*, 9/2/1968). A growing scale of business enterprise implies that, with respect to commercial relationships at least, there is growing interdependence between enterprise and environment.

Third, technical progress is associated with closer relations between business enterprises and governmental agencies. This is a most significant development, to which Galbraith (1967) and British commentators have given prominence (e.g. Jones, 1965; Hodson, 1967).[3] An indicator of this interdependence is the substantial governmental supply of R & D funds for private British industry, running as high as 75% for aircraft production, over 50% for electronics, and around 40% for scientific instruments and electrical engineering (Jones, 1965; Grossfield, 1967). Governments in all modern industrial societies consider the technically progressive growth points of industry to be quite strategic, and their educational, training and manpower policies have an obvious relation to the

---

[3] Galbraith (1967) correctly points out that this is a two-way process of influence, though his estimate of business influence over governmental agencies would be exaggerated for the British situation (cf. Rogow and Shore, 1955; Finer, 1956; Hodson, 1967), and is probably overstated for the United States as well. For the situation in Soviet Russia see Chapter III above.

course of innovation (Stieber, 1966, Part III; Stettner, 1966). Moreover, in Britain the government has followed the Italian precedent and established an Industrial Reorganization Corporation in order actively to promote industrial rationalization, partly as an improved basis for innovatory progress. Moves taken by the I.R.C., which represent a substantial new factor in the industrial power system, have certainly not all met with unqualified approval from business quarters (cf. *The Observer*, 16/6/1968; House of Commons Parliamentary Debates 8/7/1968).

It is very difficult to say how this growing interdependence between the business enterprise and its environment will affect business power in modern industrial society, since it is insufficient to adopt a position of naïve technical determinism. Thus tendencies in favour of enhanced business power consequent on technical progress—such as increased product differentiation, growing scale, and the displacement of labour—can all be offset by relevant governmental policies, as well as by action on the part of trade unions and consumer organizations. The degree of 'countervailing' control currently exercised over business would seem very roughly to increase as one moves from the United States, to the Common Market countries, to Britain and then to Communist societies. Certainly in Britain under the Labour government, commentators have pointed to a substantially increased public intervention in industry often ostensibly on issues connected with technical progress (Davies, 1967; Hodson, 1967; Shanks, 1967; Wray, 1968).

3 TECHNICAL PROGRESS, ORGANIZATION AND WORK EXPERIENCE WITHIN THE BUSINESS ENTERPRISE

When considering the organizational implications of technical progress it becomes very necessary to distinguish not only between product innovation and technological innovation, but also between the different forms which the latter can take. Even if we restrict the scope of technological innovation to 'automation', there are different types of automation varying both in levels of 'automaticity' (Amber & Amber, 1962; Auerhan, 1966) and in type of application. Applications may comprise 'Detroit automation' involving an extension of mechanization through transfer-devices;[4] automatic control over manufacturing processes; individual multi-purpose electronically controlled machines; and office automation (cf. D.S.I.R., 1956; Stettner, 1966; J. Rose, 1967).

There is so far in the literature considerable agreement on the features associated with rapid and successful product innovation (Burns & Stalker, 1961; Lawrence & Lorsch, 1967; Hage & Aiken, 1968). These include the employment of appropriate technical specialists, a limited specification of jobs and procedures, a willingness to rely on functional expertise in the shaping of decisions (involving decentralized decision-making at least on operational problems), and organizational devices whereby specialist contributions are appropriately co-ordinated (such as Burns and Stalker's 'organismic system' or Lawrence and Lorsch's 'integrative devices').[5] While persons closely concerned with rapid product innovation seem typically to feel a high involvement in their work, the pressures imposed by change and perhaps the loosely-structured type of organization that suits change are conducive to frequent inter-personal conflict and even to considerable personal anxiety and stress.

A substantial amount of writing is now available on the social consequences of technological innovation, much of it concentrated on the subject of automation. However, as Sadler (1968) has pointed out in his useful short review of social research on automation, a good deal of this writing is speculative and more detailed research remains to be done. The short-term consequences of technological innovation in many cases detract from employees' quality of work experience because of the strains and other costs involved in re-training, redeployment, domestic adjustment to shift-working, and the like. Its longer-term implications appear to vary with

[4] It can be argued that this is not true 'automation' in the sense of involving self regulation via cybernated control.

[5] Harvey (1968), studying rates of product change in 45 US industrial organizations, found an association between high rate of product change and low 'program specification' (which he claims comes close to Burns and Stalker's 'organismic' system), but not between high product change and high specialization. However, one cannot tell from the way Harvey presents his data whether specialization has been independently influenced by organizational size. Other research has found a close relation between specialization and size (cf. Pugh *et al.*, 1969).

the kind of technological innovations in question, as can be seen in the case of automation.

The most completely automated manufacturing operations are those of a process type. Process production tends to allow for (i) small, relatively autonomous work groups, (ii) an improved physical work environment, (iii) less specialized, less arduous and less closely supervised tasks which require the exercise of new conceptual and perceptual skills, (iv) more harmonious labour relations, and (v) a relatively large, specialized, and possibly more centralized management structure (P.E.P., 1957; Crossman, 1960; Mann & Hoffman, 1960; Emery & Marek, 1962; Blauner, 1964; Woodward, 1965; Hickson *et al.*, 1969). These features are strictly speaking only consequences of the type of management policy which process production makes economically feasible. The technology itself merely sets economic limits to the choice of management policy. Thus process technology may allow for the creation of close social relations in small groups in, say, a central process control room; *but* the corollary is that process control is sufficiently flexible also to allow for widely separated control points at which employees might become socially isolated and experience considerable boredom.

In contrast to process automation, single multi-purpose electronically-controlled machines are suited to small batch production, while 'Detroit automation' particularly fits mass production technology. Their implications for organization and work experience may therefore be quite different from those of process technology (Woodward, 1965; Burack, 1967). For example, Faunce (1958) found that the introduction of transfer machines into a mass production technology resulted in a less satisfying work experience because there was more personal isolation, a greater pace of work, more pressure from supervisors, and increased strain due to the need constantly to monitor costly equipment with which the whole production line was integrated.

Any discussion on the implications of automation should therefore bear two points in mind. First, the type of automation in question has to be clearly established. Secondly, one is dealing with a socio-technical system and there is normally some choice available with respect to the specification of jobs, the design of organization and other structured elements in the social system that is linked with an automated technology. In the light of these points, Naville's view (1961, 1963) that automation is leading to a new form of alienation from work seems to be over-pessimistic. For this thesis implies a technological determinism which we have already called into question, while Naville has classed as 'automation' some technologies which only amount to mechanization (e.g. Naville & Palierne, 1960).

Office automation is likely to have a greater impact on the structure of organization and power in a business enterprise than any other type of technological innovation. This is particularly true when computerized information processing is used not merely to automate existing clerical routines but to place the information, planning and control systems of an enterprise on a qualitatively new and integrated basis. Once this stage is achieved (and these new systems are now being installed in large enterprises), most commentators agree that certain routine clerical departments may disappear, traditional workflow departmental boundaries will no longer be meaningful, middle management jobs will become more routine and have a reduced discretionary content, and the managerial hierarchy will become shortened. However, this last development is by no means likely to represent an increase in middle management power. On the contrary, since information can now be standardized and since the enhanced quality of information reduces its ambiguity, decision-making is likely to become more centralized at the top of the enterprise hierarchy, to which level information can be delivered directly. Computer personnel and certain other technical experts who may previously have been on the fringes of management will tend to assume positions of considerable strategic importance with advanced computerization. These various developments may well promote conflict between technical staff and middle management, particularly during the installation of new systems (Anshen, 1962; Mann, 1962; Whisler & Shultz, 1962; Mumford & Ward, 1965; Scott, 1965; Eastwood, 1966; Stettner, 1966; Whisler, 1966; Zalewski, 1966; J. Rose, 1967; Brown, 1968; Rhee, 1968).

The 'logic' of advanced information systems would appear to extend the routinization, indeed 'bureaucratization', of work to clerical and even managerial levels where this may hitherto have been absent. This creates new differentiations of power and status between middle management and the top stratum of decision-makers, as well as further enhancing the differentiation between increasingly routinized clerical roles concerned with preparing computer input or output and increasingly responsible computer systems and programming roles. With these role differentiations new barriers to promotion will probably also arise (Leavitt & Whisler, 1958; Nehnevajsa, 1959; Mann, 1962; Mumford & Ward, 1965; Simon, 1965).[6] In other words, new locations of 'social cleavage' (Collins *et al.*, 1946) are introduced within the business enterprise, while the increasing similarity of clerical organizational roles to those of many shop floor grades may encourage clerks to shift their industrial perspectives and modes of industrial action closer to those of blue-collar employees (cf. Goldthorpe & Lockwood, 1963). Employees who have high expectations of promotion or of varied, responsible work, and whose opportunities to fulfil such expectations are reduced by advanced computerization, may well experience increased job dissatisfaction and enjoy a generally diminished quality of work experience (Mumford & Banks, 1967).

Clearly this analysis has omitted the possibilities of deliberately conceived policies to offset the 'logic' of innovation. The scope for such policies may in fact be quite dramatic if, for example, we accept the view of one commentator that advanced information systems make top decision-making even more straight-forward than he claims it already is (Foster, 1963). If there is going to be so little foundation to the 'mystique' of top management, then one of the most often quoted objections to workers' control will become progressively eroded.[7]

[6] Galbraith (1967) argues that in larger US enterprises much decision-making power has already passed from top management to technical experts, among which data processing staff are an important category. On this point (and several others) Galbraith's case appears to be exaggerated and is unsupported by hard evidence (cf. Miliband's critique, 1968).

[7] It is fair to point out that Foster's view about the demands of top decision-making under advanced computerization is not universally shared. Cf. Stettner (1966, p. 469).

4 TECHNICAL PROGRESS AND SOCIAL WELFARE

Probably more attention has been given to the consequences of technical progress—especially of automation—for employment than for any other aspect of social welfare. Diebold (1952) has taken the 'optimistic' view that the spread of automation will not lead to a significant reduction in the overall level of employment; Pollock (1957) is far more pessimistic on this issue. In spite of their very different premises, both classical and Marxist economic theories agree that technological innovations need not create unemployment in an economy as a whole. It has, however, become clear that in both western and communist societies serious employment problems can arise. Certainly one of the main reasons for introducing technological innovation may be to displace labour in order to improve the quantity and/or quality of work performed relative to costs. Through creating redundancies and altering requisite patterns of skill, technological innovation (and sometimes product innovation) presents important social problems especially for certain groups of employees whose adaptability may be low due to age, lack of education and so on. Even in communist societies, where redundancy is not officially recognized as a problem with their 'full employment' economies, employees are sometimes kept on the payrolls of enterprises which no longer require their services until they can be absorbed elsewhere (Buckingham, 1961; Chapter 6; Clague & Greenberg, 1962; Stieber, 1966, Part II; Stettner, 1966).[8]

There is a popular expectation that technical progress in industry will through more mechanization and automation open up a new era of the leisured society. It would certainly

[8] (1) There is considerable debate among economists in the United States where persistently high levels of unemployment present a serious social problem, as to whether the main contributory factor to unemployment has been rapid technological innovation (creating so-called 'structural unemployment') or inadequate levels of aggregate demand due to the reluctance until recently of American governments to employ Keynesian economic regulators. Cf. Stieber (1966), Chapters 7 & 8. (2) It is also worth noting that a further social cost may be inflicted by technological innovation if it leads to increased industrial conflict over the issue of redundancy. Cf. Stettner (1966, p. 476).

appear socially desirable for businessmen and trade unionists to agree upon shorter working hours rather than on redundancies as their reaction to technological innovation, but economic factors tend to militate against this. There are in fact few signs that average hours actually worked in modern industrial societies (in manufacturing industry at least) have dramatically declined over the past 10 years or so. Indeed, in the highly prosperous and technologically advanced economies of Canada and the United States hours worked have shown a rising trend (UN 1967, p. 107). Average hours worked per week in Britain were the same in 1958 as in 1938, and only marginally less in 1966 (Boston, 1968).[9]

Technical progress in the business enterprise does carry some implications for the quality of people's leisure. Thus heavy capital investment in technological innovation enhances the economies of shift working which may have deprivating consequences for leisure opportunities (Hoos, 1960, 1961; Aris, 1964; Mott *et al.*, 1965). Where technological innovation is of a kind that sets up greater personal stress, employees may keenly desire the extra leisure it makes possible (Faunce, 1959). Friedman (1964), who shares Naville's view that automation at best seems to offer no mitigation of the problem of alienation at work, argues that as a result the central life interests of many employees is moving towards the non-work sphere. The implications of different forms of innovation for the functions served by leisure time form part of the work-leisure nexus which, as we concluded in Chapter IV, requires much further research.

Another question which needs more investigation is the effect of innovation within business enterprises upon social

[9] Stettner (1966) writes of a 'dramatic reduction of work hours in the past decade, in all parts of the industrialized world' which is 'a direct consequence of technological progress' (p. 473). We argue that this is a considerable overstatement, although technological innovation may have reduced work hours in some industries or occupations. An explanation for only a slow or even non-existent decline in average work hours in a society is forthcoming if one considers (1) that technological innovation is not spread evenly through all industries and affects some rather slightly, and (2) that employees themselves may not wish to work shorter hours if this means a cut in their total remuneration (Neuloh, 1966, p. 208). Indeed they may take advantage of a reduction of working hours in one job to earn more by taking another job (cf. Wilensky, 1963). Technological determinism cannot account for point (2).

stratification in modern industrial societies. Goldthorpe (1964) has argued that a comparison of western and communist industrial societies does not permit us to adopt an explanation of social stratification simply in terms of economic and technological determinism. However, leaving aside the independent effects of different socio-cultural environments and policies, one may still ask what implications industrial innovation poses for social stratification. In this connection, both product and technological innovation are associated with a relative expansion in scientific and technical grades of employment. Technological innovation also tends to promote the relative increase in white collar compared with manual employees which has been evident in recent decades (cf. Dill, 1965, p. 1087; Knight, 1967, p. 410; *Growth of Office Employment*, 1968).[10] The automation of manual work (apart from the Detroit type) tends to create jobs of higher responsibility carrying higher remuneration and less opportunity for mass shopfloor social groupings. Consequences such as these have led some to conclude that technical progress is weakening workers' traditional social ties (Moos, 1964), and that it is leading to a 'professional society' in which class differences are becoming less visible and status is increasingly deriving from skill and education rather than organizational position (Faunce & Clelland, 1963; Faunce, 1968, Chapter 4).

In contrast is the view that technological innovation has already in the United States opened up a gap in society between the employed and the 'unemployables' whose abilities do not match current requirements (Ferry, 1965). We have also noted the prediction that new information technology will increase intra-organizational differentiation. If this is associated with separate meritocratic channels of occupational entry and reduced inter-generational social mobility, then increasingly rigid social stratification seems to be implied. In this respect, Young's warnings on 'the rise of the meritocracy' (1958) are being borne out by trends in managerial recruitment which indicate a growing restriction of entry to people possessing a technical or higher education (Warner & Abegglen, 1955; Acton Society Trust, 1956; Clements, 1958; Clark, 1966; Clark & Mosson, 1967; Richman, 1967). And if the

[10] Even with office automation, net clerical redundancies have often been quite small—Scott (1965).

current trend towards industrial concentration and large-scale enterprises is accompanied—as predicted—by increasingly centralized decision-making in such enterprises as integrated information systems are adopted, then social differentiation will again be furthered with respect, this time, to the distribution of power. The feeling that power is becoming increasingly centralized in society is very possibly the main factor behind recent demands for participation and devolution of decision-making which have been evident in most industrial societies.

We do not wish to suggest that any of these social implications of technical progress are inevitable. Indeed, the demand for revised structural arrangements contained in requests for participation is, as we argued in the previous chapter, one which it may be possible to accommodate further in industry without detriment to economic performance. The fact that technical progress can be regulated and utilized to accord with the social values and political policies of the society in question (or of its ruling group) is a point which has been overlooked by those who predict a necessary 'convergence' between the forms of business enterprise and its environment to be found in modern industrial societies.

5 BUSINESS ENTERPRISE AND SOCIETY— CONVERGING MODELS?

The argument that economic and associated technological forces cause social structures to pass through similar stages of development culminating in the same structural configuration is primarily associated with Marx's writings (Bottomore & Rubel, 1956, Part I). There is today wide support for Popper's view (1957) that historicist theories of this kind can and should be refuted. However, quite recently, evidence of certain similarities in the economic, organizational and technological problems faced by business enterprise in modern industrial societies possessing ostensibly quite different political ideologies has encouraged an emergence of the so-called 'convergence thesis'.[11]

---

[11] One should perhaps say 're-emergence' for it will be seen that the convergence thesis possesses striking parallels with Marx's thesis of societal convergence towards the single communist model as industrialization proceeds.

Simply put, the convergence thesis holds that the processes of industrialization give rise to structural constraints which in turn make for convergent patterns of social development in all modern industrial societies. These economically determined common patterns are seen as inevitable regardless of prevailing social ideologies and cultural values, and indeed it is expected that ideology will be re-shaped in accordance with underlying economic forces (again cf. Marx). The convergence thesis does not claim that social patterns in modern industrial societies are similar, but rather that they are becoming more alike. In addition, there are several different expositions of the thesis ranging between what Dunning and Hopper (1966) have called 'total' and 'partial' patterns of change, or 'one-way' and 'two-way' directions of change.[12] The thesis has normally been applied to the current and future developments of advanced capitalist and communist systems, particularly the USA and USSR.

Convergence theorists point out that at given stages of economic development certain similarities occur with respect to business organization (such as economies of scale, optimum production functions) and with respect to the social concomitants of successful business performance, both permissive (such as effective resource allocation, demand management, and provision of suitably qualified manpower) and consequential (such as the distribution of rewards, or social adjustments to technological innovation). These common opportunities and problems set up pressures, it is argued, towards the adoption of similar forms of business enterprise and economic regulation. But at this point differences in the argument begin to appear.

Thus Richman (1965) adopts a moderate and largely 'one-way' convergence standpoint. He suggests that the USSR will be obliged by the growing complexity of its economic system to adopt some of the features of the more advanced American economy—particularly, resource allocation guided by price-registered scarcities and enterprise planning largely decentra-

---

[12] A 'total' pattern of change, in the context of convergence, means that all structural elements in societies are converging; a 'partial' pattern of change means that only some elements are converging. 'One-way' convergence implies that one model is moving closer to another which remains essentially the same (e.g. Communism moving closer to Capitalism); 'two-way' convergence implies that both models are moving closer together towards some common pattern.

lized to the level of enterprise management. However, Richman clearly appreciates that the ideological traditions and vested interests of the Soviet Communist Party will probably not permit any such changes to progress as far as a full market allocative system (p. 240), and indeed it is clear that the Soviet leadership is treading but slowly and reluctantly along the road to such changes (Nove, 1968a; 1968b).

In his 1964 Reith Lectures, Sir Leon Bagrit (1964)[13] expressed the much less guarded view that the differences between Capitalism and Communism were beginning to diminish primarily because of the consequences of advancing automation. He argued that a new 'technological class' emerged in step with this trend. This class had no time for party politics based on old clichés and as a result Bagrit foresaw the amendment, if not crumbling, of orthodox political theories which were inadequate to cope with the vast problems produced by the new technology. Bagrit's comments on the emergence of a new technocratic elite in the USSR which is unsympathetic towards prevailing political ideology and the party bureaucracy have been echoed by other students of the contemporary Russian scene such as Garder (1965), Tatu (1965) and Parry (1966).

In *his* 1966 Reith Lectures (1966), subsequently amplified into *The New Industrial State* (1967), Galbraith greatly extended Bagrit's technologically based and 'two-way' convergence thesis. Galbraith has argued that the application of modern science to industry has greatly enhanced the complexity of business planning in all industrial societies. As a result, the salaried specialist staff of an enterprise—its 'technostructure'—has to be accorded considerable, and increasing, autonomy for the enterprise to function at all effectively. Therefore despite 'public ritual' suggesting the contrary, control over the enterprise in capitalist societies is passing from legal ownership to its salaried managers, and is being devolved from the state to managers in communist societies. Moreover, Galbraith asserts that the common requirements of business in both types of society are promoting increasingly similar national policies with regard to ensuring adequate purchasing power to absorb industrial products or a supply of trained manpower adequate for business requirements. In short, 'convergence between the two ostensibly different

[13] Then Chairman of Elliott-Automation Ltd.

industrial systems occurs at all fundamental points' (1967, p. 391).

An even more far-reaching version of the convergence thesis is that formulated by some American sociologists, most explicitly by Kerr and his associates (1960). This version sees a 'logic' of industrialism as promoting, even compelling, the emergence not just of a new type of economic system, but of a new type of society. Progress to this new model of society represents a two-way convergence[14] from former 'class' and 'mass' models towards a single 'pluralistic' model of multiple interest groups competing within a set of rules regulated by the state. Goldthorpe (1964) has reviewed this convergence approach with particular reference to its conclusions on social stratification in modern industrial society.

There are several comments to make on the foregoing arguments, which have concerned a strategic area of current sociological enquiry. First, as Meade (1968) and Miliband (1968) have indicated, the extent of present similarities between American and Russian business systems has been greatly overstated, especially by Galbraith. For instance, Galbraith equates far too readily the American mode of economic planning decentralized at enterprise level with the centrally directed planning of the USSR. The two systems of planning are quite different. Second, the question of convergence relates to longitudinal economic and social developments, and any assessment is rendered extremely difficult because adequate historical data is not available particularly for communist societies. One returns here to the problem of defining an industrial society which is a prerequisite to finding appropriate comparative indices. For example, to take a criterion we mentioned in Chapter I, similar percentages of working populations engaged in non-agricultural occupations do not necessarily indicate that different societies are industrially equally advanced in terms of, say, applied technical progress.

On the basis of our present knowledge there is no reason to predict anything like a complete or consistent convergence between industrial societies (Feldman & Moore, 1965; Moore,

---

[14] A 'two-way unequal convergence' in that Kerr *et al.* (1960) appear to envisage communist societies becoming more like their 'ideal typical' model of American society rather than vice versa (Goldthorpe, 1966b, p. 188).

1965; Chapter 2). At the level of the business enterprise we have already noted (Chapter V) how there is scope for organizational variation within any limits set by the goal of economic effectiveness. Even mediating features such as size and technology are not at all rigidly determined by business environment. And an independent factor in the equation for economic effectiveness is the culturally defined expectations of employees which, if not satisfied, can induce costly absenteeism and labour turnover, or poor quality work. For this kind of reason alone, socio-cultural differences are likely to continue as a factor making for variation in forms of business organization (cf. Chapter II). Indeed, there is no good evidence that different value-systems are ceasing to leave their stamp upon social institutions, as Goldthorpe (1964) and Platt (1964) have indicated with regard to social stratification in capitalist and communist societies, and Shonfield (1965) with regard to key institutions and economic policies even within otherwise somewhat similar post-war capitalist societies.

In short, the convergence thesis has usefully pointed to certain similarities in the economic structures of modern industrial societies. It has, however, exaggerated their sociological consequence and it has understated the counter-acting role of purposive policies which are shaped in accord with different national cultures and prevailing ideologies. The convergence thesis is an aspect of the 'end of ideology' theme in modern sociology which has been assessed aptly as 'a perspective that is profoundly conservative and [itself] altogether an ideology' (Abrams, 1963, p. 30). The convergence thesis, expressed in its balder Galbraithian forms, not only amounts to a conservative apologetic for the 'needs' of a capitalist business system (as Miliband, 1968 has argued); it is also a conservative view on the opportunities available to control and shape the business enterprise and its role in modern industrial society as we may wish. The research which was reviewed in the later chapters of this book belies a conservative standpoint. For it encourages the expectation that an expansion of scientific sociological investigation into the nature of business enterprises will make possible an increasingly sophisticated approach to organizational design which will allow us the better to satisfy our economic and social priorities.

Bibliography

The references which are annotated and marked with an asterisk have been selected as suggestions for further reading on the topics covered in this book.

AARONOVITCH, S. (1955). *Monopoly: A Study of British Monopoly Capitalism.* London: Lawrence & Wishart.

AARONOVITCH, S. (1961). *The Ruling Class.* London: Lawrence & Wishart.

* ABEGGLEN, J. C. (1958). *The Japanese Factory.* Glencoe, Ill.: Free Press. Describes the major organizational features of Japanese enterprise, including recruitment procedures, and links these to characteristics of Japanese society.

* ABRAHAMSON, M. (1967). *The Professional in the Organization.* Chicago: Rand McNally. Selection of readings relating to a wide variety of organizational situations.

ABRAMS, P. (1963). 'New Lamps for Old: Some Thoughts on the End of Ideology', in K. NEWTON (ed.), *Cambridge Opinion,* 34: 25–30.

ACTON SOCIETY TRUST (1953, 1957). *Size and Morale.* London: The Trust. Pt. I, 1953, Pt. II, 1957.

ACTON SOCIETY TRUST (1956). *Management Succession.* London: The Trust.

ADORNO, T. W., FRENKEL-BRUNSWIK, E., LEVINSON, D. J. and SANFORD, R. N. (1950). *The Authoritarian Personality.* New York: Harper.

* AIKEN, M. and HAGE, J. (1966). 'Organizational Alienation: A Comparative Analysis', *American Sociological Review,* 31, 4, Aug.: 497–507. Relationships between two types of alienation and organizational centralization and formalization studied comparatively in sixteen American welfare organizations.

AIKEN, M. and HAGE, J. (1967). *Organizational Structure and Interorganizational Dynamics,* paper read at the annual meeting of the American Sociological Association, Aug. (mimeographed).

* ALBROW, M. (1968). 'The Study of Organizations—Objectivity or Bias?' in J. GOULD (ed.), *Penguin Social Sciences Survey 1968,* Harmondsworth: Penguin, 146–67. Argues that it is invalid to identify the sociological approach to the study of organizations with organization theory.

* ALLEN, G. C. (1966). *The Structure of Industry in Britain.* London: Longmans, 2nd edition. Useful concise review.

* ALLEN, G. C. (1967). *Economic Fact and Fantasy: A Rejoinder to Professor Galbraith's Reith Lectures,* London: Institute of Economic Affairs, Occasional Paper 14. Stimulating critique of J. K. Galb-

raith's 1966 Reith Lectures (c.f., *The New Industrial State* 1967).

ALLEN, G. C. (1968). *Monopoly and Restrictive Practices*. London: Allen & Unwin.

AMBER, G. S. and AMBER, P. S. (1962). *Anatomy of Automation*. Englewood Cliffs, N.J.: Prentice-Hall.

AMES, E. (1961). 'Research, Invention, Development and Innovation', communication to *American Economic Review*, LI: 370–81.

ANDERSON, P. and BLACKBURN, R. (1965)—(eds.), *Towards Socialism*. London: Fontana.

ANDRESKI, S. (1964). 'The Idea of Industrial Society: A Comment', in *The Development of Industrial Societies*, Sociological Review Monograph No. 8, University of Keele: 13–14.

Annual Abstract of Statistics (1968). No. 105, London: H.M.S.O.

ANSHEN, M. (1962). 'Managerial Decisions', in J. T. DUNLOP (ed.), *Automation and Technological Change*. Englewood Cliffs, N.J.: Prentice-Hall: 66–83.

* ARENSBURG, C. M. (1942). 'Industry and the Community', *American Journal of Sociology*, XLVIII, 1, July: 1–12. Argues the need for more study of the relationships between industrial enterprises and their community environments, unifying inter-disciplinary research within a sociological conception of 'the continuum of industry and the community.'

ARGYLE, M. (1957). *The Scientific Study of Social Behaviour*. London: Methuen.

* ARGYRIS, C. (1957). *Personality and Organization: The Conflict Between System and Individual*. New York: Harper & Row. The first, and perhaps best, of a series of works in which Argyris explores the conflict between formal administrative structure and the needs of psychologically mature individuals.

* ARGYRIS, C. (1958). 'The Organization: What makes it Healthy?' *Harvard Business Review*, 36, 6, Nov.–Dec.: 107–16. Case study indicating considerable employee non-involvement with the enterprise. Argyris considers that such employees sign a 'psychological work contract', exchanging satisfaction at work for a high wage to buy satisfaction elsewhere.

ARGYRIS, C. (1960). *Understanding Organizational Behavior*. Homewood, Ill.: Dorsey Press.

ARGYRIS, C. (1962). 'The Integration of the Individual and the Organization', in G. B. STROTHER (ed), *Social Science Approaches to Business Behavior*. London: Tavistock: Chapter 2.

ARGYRIS, C. (1964). *Integrating the Individual and the Organization*. New York: Wiley.

ARIS, S. (1964). 'The Future of Shift Work', *New Society*. 2nd Jan: 8–10.

* ARMSTRONG, A. and SILBERSTON, A. (1965). 'Size of Plant, Size of Enterprise and Concentration in British Manufacturing Industry 1935–58', *Journal of the Royal Statistical Society*, Series A, 128, 3: 395–420. Analysis of Census of Production Data.

* ARMSTRONG, J. A. (1965). 'Sources of Administrative Behavior: Some Soviet and Western European Comparisons', *American Political Science Review*, LIX, 3, Sept.: 643–55. Describes similarities and differences between Soviet and Western European administrative behaviour, and discusses their sources. Data from interviews with 61 administrators from W. Germany, Britain and France who had visited the U.S.S.R.

ASHTON, T. S. (1948). *The Industrial Revolution 1760–1830*. London: Oxford University Press.

AUERHAN, J. (1966). 'Technological Change in the Socialist Countries', in J. STIEBER (ed.), *Employment Problems of Automation and Advanced Technology*. London: Macmillan 32–47.

* BAGRIT, SIR LEON (1964). 1964 Reith Lectures on 'Automation: An Extension of Man'—Lecture No. 5, reported in *The Listener*, LXXII, 10th Dec. Argues that the impact of automation is diminishing differences between capitalist and communist societies.

BAIN, J. S. (1959). *Industrial Organization*. New York: Wiley.

* BALDWIN, W. L. (1964). 'The Motives of Managers, Environmental Restraints and the Theory of Managerial Enterprise', *Quarterly Journal of Economics*, LXXVIII, 2, May: 238–56. If we want a theory of managerial enterprise which assumes a single organizational objective, then profit appears to be more realistic than any of the alternatives so far offered.

BANKS, J. A. (1963a). Review of A. K. Rice (1963). 'The Enterprise and its Environment', *Sociological Review*, 11: 374–5.

BANKS, J. A. (1963b). *Industrial Participation—Theory and Practice: A Case Study*. Liverpool: University Press.

* BARAN, P. A. and SWEEZY, P. M. (1966). *Monopoly Capital: An Essay on the American Economic and Social Order*. New York: Monthly Review Press. Marxist analysis of trends in the contemporary American economic and social system. Contains a chapter on 'The Giant Corporation'.

BARKIN, S. (1965). 'The Decline of the Labor Movement', in A. HACKER (ed.), *The Corporation Take-Over*. New York: Doubleday, Chapter 11.

BARNARD, C. I. (1938). *The Functions of the Executive*. Cambridge, Mass.: Harvard University Press.

BARRATT-BROWN, M. (1958–9). 'The Controllers', *Universities and Left Review*, Autumn 1958, Spring & Autumn 1959.

BARRON, M. J. (1967). 'The Effect of the Size of the Firm on Profitability', *Business Ratios*, 1, Spring: 13–15.

BARTH, E. A. T. (1963). 'The Causes and Consequences of Interagency Conflict', *Sociological Inquiry*, 33, Winter: 51–7.

BASSOUL, R., BERNARD, P. and TOURAINE, A. (1960). 'Retrait, Conflit, Participation: Trois Types d'Attitudes Ouvrières au Travail', *Sociologie du Travail*, II, 4, Oct.–Dec.: 314–29.

BAUMOL, W. J. (1967). *Business Behavior, Value and Growth*, revised ed., New York: Harcourt Brace.

BECKER, H. S. and CARPER, J. (1956). 'The Elements of Identification with an Occupation', *American Sociological Review*, 21, June: 341–8.

* BEED, C. S. (1966). 'The Separation of Ownership from Control', *The Journal of Economic Studies*, 1, 2, Summer: 29–46. An important critique of the methodology employed by Berle and Means in *The Modern Corporation and Private Property* (q.v.). Concludes that despite the influence of Berle and Means' thesis, the ownership and control issue is far from resolved.

BEHREND, H. (1957). 'The Effort-Bargain', *Industrial and Labor Relations Review*, 10, 4: 503–15.

BELL, D. (1961). *The End of Ideology*. New York: Collier Books.

BENDIX, R. (1945). 'Bureaucracy and the Problem of Power', *Public Administration Review*, V: 194–209.

* BENDIX, R. (1956). *Work and Authority in Industry: Ideologies of Management in the Course of Industrialization*. New York: Wiley. Examination of managerial ideologies in early English industrialization, Tsarist Russia, modern America and East Germany; also their historical sources and social consequences. Contains a section on the 'Bureaucratization of Economic Enterprises'.

* BERLE, A. A. (1954). *The Twentieth Century Capitalist Revolution*. New York: Harcourt Brace. On the problem of corporate power. Berle sees this as being regulated and limited through a corporate 'conscience' activated by public pressures.

BERLE, A. A. (1957). *Economic Power and the Free Society*. New York. (Fund for the Republic Pamphlet.)

* BERLE, A. A. (1959a). *Power Without Property—A New Development in American Political Economy*. New York: Harcourt Brace. Analyses the modern American economy as a system of 'peoples' capitalism'.

BERLE, A. A. (1959b). 'Foreword' to E. S. MASON (ed.), *The Corporation in Modern Society*. Cambridge, Mass.: Harvard University Press.

* BERLE, A. A. and MEANS, G. C. (1932). *The Modern Corporation and Private Property*. New York: Macmillan. Classic exposition of the thesis that ownership and control are separated in modern large business enterprises. Raises questions of managerial power and responsibility which Berle explores further in more recent works.

* BERLINER, J. S. (1957). *Factory and Manager in the U.S.S.R.* Cambridge, Mass.: Harvard University Press. Pioneering study based on interviews with Russian emigrés.

BERNSTEIN, M. H. (1955). *Regulating Business by Independent Commission*. Princeton, N.J.: Princeton University Press.

VON BERTALANFFY, L. (1950). 'The Theory of Open Systems in Physics and Biology', *Science*, III: 23–9.

BESCOBY, J. and TURNER, H. A. (1961). 'An Analysis of Post-War Labour Disputes in the British Car-Manufacturing Firms', *The Manchester School of Economics and Social Studies*. May: 133–60.

BIRMAN, A. (1968). 'The Third Year of Reform: Production Figures Point to the Success of the New System', *Financial Times*, Survey on Soviet

Industry, 6th Aug.: 16–17.

* BIRNBAUM, N. (1964). 'The Idea of Industrial Society', in *The Development of Industrial Societies,* Sociological Review Monograph no. 8, University of Keele: 5–12. Discusses the main themes associated with the pioneering analyses of industrial societies by Marx, De Tocqueville and Weber.

BLACKBURN, R. (1965). 'The New Capitalism', in P. ANDERSON and R. BLACKBURN (eds.). *Towards Socialism.* London: Fontana: 114–45.

BLACKETT, P. M. S. (1968). 'Are R & D Teams Big Enough for the Job? *The Times,* 26th July: 19.

* BLAU, P. M. *and* SCOTT, W. G. (1963). *Formal Organizations.* London: Routledge & Kegan Paul. A typology of organizations by prime beneficiary is derived as part of a theoretical treatment adopting a comparative approach aimed at generalizations about organizational structure and dynamics.

BLAUNER, R. (1960). 'Work Satisfaction and Industrial Trends in Modern Society', in W. GALENSON and S. M. LIPSET (eds.), *Labor and Trade Unionism.* New York: Wiley: 339–60.

* BLAUNER, R. (1964). *Alienation and Freedom: The Factory Worker and His Industry.* Chicago: University of Chicago Press. Study of four American industries representing different stages of technological development. Concludes that alienation of factory workers varies with technological differences, and therefore urges sociologists to note the diversity of work situations found in industry.

BLEASE, J. G. (1964). 'Institutional Investors and the Stock Exchange', *District Bank Review,* 151, Sept.: 38–64.

* BLUMBERG, P. (1968). *Industrial Democracy: The Sociology of Participation.* London: Constable. An important, detailed review of evidence on various forms of employee participation in decision-making. Concludes that participation is preferable to other suggested remedies for work alienation.

* BODDEWYN, J. (1967). 'The Analysis of Business Systems and their Environment', *University of Washington Business Review,* XXVI, 4, Summer: 68–79. Discusses the concept of business environment and presents a typology.

BOND-WILLIAMS, N. I. (1953). 'Informal Workers' Groups: An Interim Report of an Industrial Experiment', *British Management Review,* XI, 4, July: 37–56.

BORDEN, N. H. (1942). *The Economic Effects of Advertising.* Chicago: Irwin.

BOSTON, R. (1968). 'What Leisure?' *New Society,* 26th Dec.: 937–8.

BOTTOMORE, T. B. (1964). *Elites and Society.* London: Watts.

BOTTOMORE, T. B. and RUBEL, M. (1956)—(eds.). *Karl Marx: Selected Writings in Sociology and Social Philosophy.* London: Watts.

BOULDING, K. E. (1953). *The Organizational Revolution.* New York: Harper.

BOWEN, H. R. (1953). *Social Responsibilities of the Businessman*. New York: Harper.

BOX, S. and COTGROVE, S. (1966). 'Scientific Identity, Occupational Selection and Role Strain', *British Journal of Sociology*, XVII, 1, March: 20–8.

BRITT, S. H. (1966). *Consumer Behavior and the Behavioral Sciences: Theories and Applications*, New York: Wiley.

BROWN, M. (1966). *On the Theory and Measurement of Technological Change*, Cambridge: The University Press.

BROWN, R. K. (1967). 'Research and Consultancy in Industrial Enterprises: A Review of the Contribution of the Tavistock Institute of Human Relations to the Development of Industrial Sociology', *Sociology*, 1, 1, Jan.: 33–60.

BROWN, R. K. (1968). 'Technology, Technical Change and Automation', in S. R. PARKER, R. K. BROWN, J. CHILD and M. A. SMITH, *The Sociology of Industry*. London: Allen & Unwin.

BROWN, R. K. and BRANNEN, P. (1968). 'Homogeneity and Diversity among Ship-Building Workers', paper read at *S.S.R.C. Conference on 'Social Stratification and Industrial Relations'*, Cambridge, Sept. (mimeographed).

BROWN, W. (1960). *Exploration in Management*. London: Heinemann.

BUCKINGHAM, W. (1961). *Automation, Its Impact on Business and People*. New York: Harper.

BURACK, E. H. (1967). 'Industrial Management in Advanced Production Systems: Some Theoretical Concepts and Preliminary Findings', *Administrative Science Quarterly*, 12, 3, Dec.: 479–500.

* BURNHAM, J. (1941). *The Managerial Revolution*. New York: Day. Popularized the notion of a managerial revolution, but his analysis has since been heavily criticized.

BURNS, T. (1964a). 'Technology', in J. GOULD and W. L. KOLB (eds.), *A Dictionary of the Social Sciences*. New York: Free Press 716–17.

BURNS, T. (1964b). 'What Managers Do', *New Society*, 17th Dec.: 8–9.

BURNS, T. (1966a). 'The Study of Consumer Behaviour—A Sociological View', *European Journal of Sociology*, VII, 2: 313–29.

* BURNS, T. (1966b). 'On the Plurality of Social Systems', in J. R. LAWRENCE (ed.), *Operational Research and the Social Sciences*, London: Tavistock, 165–77. Analysis of social systems within work organizations, and critique of the conception (found in much organization theory) of organizations as homogeneous structures.

* BURNS, T. and STALKER, G. M. (1961). *The Management of Innovation*. London: Tavistock. Research in British industry led to two types of management system being distinguished—mechanistic and organic. Which is more efficient depends on rates of change in enterprise environment, but the more flexible organic system creates personal stress and insecurity.

* CAPLOW, T. (1954). *The Sociology of Work*. New York: McGraw-Hill. Insightful sociological analysis on occupations and division of labour.

CARTWRIGHT, D. and ZANDER, A. (1960). *Group Dynamics: Research and Theory*. New York: Harper & Row. 2nd edition.

CENTERS, R. and BUGENTAL, D. E. (1966). 'Intrinsic and Extrinsic Job Motivations among Different Segments of the Working Population', *Journal of Applied Psychology*, 50, 3, June: 193–7.

CHEIT, E. F. (1964). 'The New Place of Business—Why Managers Cultivate Social Responsibility', in E. F. CHEIT (ed.), *The Business Establishment*. New York: Wiley: 152–92.

CHILD, J. (1964). 'Quaker Employers and Industrial Relations', *Sociological Review*, 12, 3, Nov.: 293–315.

CHILD, J. (1967). 'Comparative Research on Organizations', *ATM Bulletin*, VII, 5, Dec.: 1–12.

CHILD, J. (1968). 'British Management Thought as a Case Study Within the Sociology of Knowledge', *Sociological Review*, 16, 2, July: 217–39.

* CHILD, J. (1969). *British Management Thought: A Critical Analysis*. London: Allen & Unwin. Historical review utilizing perspectives of the sociology of knowledge.

CHILDS, M. W. and CATER, D. (1954). *Ethics in a Business Society*. New York: Harper.

CHINOY, E. (1955). *Automobile Workers and the American Dream*. New York: Doubleday.

CLAGUE, E. and GREENBERG, L. (1962). 'Employment', in J. T. DUNLOP (ed.), *Automation and Technological Change*. Englewood Cliffs, N.J.: Prentice-Hall: Chapter 7.

CLARK, D. G. (1966). *The Industrial Manager: His Background and Career Pattern*. London: Business Publications.

CLARK, D. G. and MOSSON, T. M. (1967). 'Industrial Managers in Belgium, France and the United Kingdom—a Comparison', *Management International*, 7, 2–3: 95–100.

CLEGG, H. A. (1960). *A New Approach to Industrial Democracy*. Oxford: Blackwell.

CLELAND, S. (1955). *The Influence of Plant Size on Industrial Relations*. Princeton University, N. J., Industrial Relations Section, Dept. of Economics and Sociology.

CLEMENTS, R. V. (1958). *Managers: A Study of their Careers in Industry*. London: Allen & Unwin.

Cmnd. 1337 (1961). *The Financial and Economic Obligations of the Nationalised Industries*. London: H.M.S.O.

Cmnd. 3437 (1967). *Nationalised Industries: A Review of Economic and Financial Objectives*. London: H.M.S.O.

COATES, K. (1965). 'Democracy and Workers' Control', in P. ANDERSON and R. BLACKBURN (eds.), *Towards Socialism*. London: Fontana: 291–316.

COCH, L. and FRENCH, J. R. P. (1948). 'Overcoming Resistance to Change', *Human Relations*, I, Aug.: 512–32.

COLLINS, O., DALTON, M. and ROY, D. (1946). 'Restriction of Output and Social Cleavage in Industry', *Applied Anthropology*, 5, Summer: 1–14.

128

CONNOCK, M. (1968). 'Productivity and Profit Incentives', *Financial Times*, Survey on Soviet Industry, 6th Aug.: 17.

COOPER, M. H. (1966). *Prices and Profits in the Pharmaceutical Industry*. Oxford: Pergamon Press.

COOPER, R. C. and PAYNE, R. L. (1967). 'Extraversion and Some Aspects of Work Behaviour', *Personnel Psychology*, 20, 1, Spring: 45–57.

CORTIS, L. E. (1962). 'A Comparative Study in the Attitudes of Bantu and European Workers', *Psychologia Africana*, 9: 148–67.

COTGROVE, S. and PARKER, S. (1963). 'Work and Non-Work', *New Society*, 11th July: 18–19.

CROSLAND, C. A. R. (1956). *The Future of Socialism*. London: Cape.

CROSLAND, C. A. R. (1959). 'The Private and Public Corporation in Great Britain', in E. S. MASON (ed.), *The Corporation in Modern Society*. Cambridge, Mass.: Harvard University Press: Chapter 13.

CROSLAND, C. A. R. (1962). *The Conservative Enemy*. London: Cape.

CROSSMAN, E. R. F. W. (1960). *Automation and Skill*. London: D.S.I.R.

* CROZIER, M. (1964). *The Bureaucratic Phenomenon*. London: Tavistock. Develops a 'strategic' model of bureaucracy by inclusion of power relationships. Sees different society-wide norms as independent variables giving rise to typically different organization structures.

* CUNNISON, S. (1966). *Wages and Work Allocation*. London: Tavistock. Empirical study which attempts to locate behaviour at work within a framework of social as well as economic environment.

* CYERT, R. M. and MARCH, J. G. (1963). *A Behavioral Theory of the Firm*. Englewood Cliffs, N.J.: Prentice-Hall. Argues for a revised analysis of the firm centering on organizational decision-making. Presents a range of new concepts and a basic structure for such an analysis.

DAHRENDORF, R. (1959). *Class and Class Conflict in Modern Society*. London: Routledge & Kegan Paul.

* DALTON, M. (1959). *Men Who Manage*. New York: Wiley. Case studies illustrating conflicts of power and political manœuvres within administrative structures of business companies.

DAS, N. (1964). *Experiments in Industrial Democracy*. New York: Asia Publishing House.

DAVIES, B. (1967). 'Some Thoughts on "Organizational Democracy"', *Journal of Management Studies*, 4, 3, Oct.: 270–81.

DAVIES, J. (1967). 'Industry and Government', *Three Banks Review*, 74, June: 16–28.

DAVIS, K. and BLOMSTROM, R. L. (1966). *Business and its Environment*. New York: McGraw-Hill.

DELAMOTTE, Y. (1959). 'Conflit Industriel et Participation Ouvrière', *Sociologie du Travail*, I, 1, Oct.–Dec.: 12–23.

DENNIS, N., HENRIQUES, F. M. and SLAUGHTER, C. (1957). *Coal is Our Life*. London: Eyre and Spottiswoode.

Department of Employment and Productivity (1968). *Statistics on Incomes, Prices, Employment and Production*, 27, Dec.: Table A 4.

Department of Scientific and Industrial Research (1956). *Automation*. London: H.M.S.O.

DERBER, M. (1963). 'Worker Participation in Israeli Management', *Industrial Relations*, 3, 1, Oct.: 51–72.

DIEBOLD, J. (1952). *Automation: The Advent of the Automatic Factory*. New York: Van Nostrand.

DILL, W. R. (1958). 'Environment as an Influence on Managerial Autonomy', *Administrative Science Quarterly*, 2: 409–43.

DILL, W. R. (1962). 'The Impact of Environment on Organizational Development', in S. MAILICK and E. H. VAN NESS (eds.), *Concepts and Issues in Administrative Behavior*. Englewood Cliffs, N.J.: Prentice-Hall, 94–109.

* DILL, W. R. (1965). 'Business Organizations', in J. G. MARCH (ed.), *Handbook of Organizations*. Chicago: Rand McNally: 1071–1114. An extensive review of research and references.

DRUCKER, P. F. (1943). *The Future of Industrial Man*. London: Heinemann.

* DRUCKER, P. F. (1946). *Concept of the Corporation*. New York: Day. (Published as *Big Business* by Heinemann, London, 1947). Refers to experience in General Motors to suggest policies whereby the activities of large corporations may be brought into closer harmony with social interests.

* DRUCKER, P. F. (1951). *The New Society*. London: Heinemann. Advances the notion of the 'self-governing plant community'.

* DUBIN, R. (1956). 'Industrial Workers' Worlds: A Study of the Central Life Interests of Industrial Workers', *Social Problems*, 3, Jan.: 131–42. Study of workers in three mid-west American plants. Found that work was not a 'central life interest' for two-thirds of them.

* DUMAZEDIER, J. (1964). 'Travail et Loisir', in G. FRIEDMANN and P. NAVILLE (eds.), *Traité de Sociologie du Travail*. Paris: Librairie Colin, revised ed., vol. II, Chapter 24. Discusses relationship between work and leisure in the light of technical progress and other social developments. Urges social scientists to take an active role in exploring possible new forms which this relationship might take.

DUN and BRADSTREET LTD. (1967). *Guide to Key British Enterprises*. London, 4th edition.

DUNNING, E. G. and HOPPER, E. I. (1966). 'Industrialisation and the Problem of Convergence: A Critical Note', *Sociological Review*, 14, 2, July: 163–86.

DUNNING J. H. (1965). 'Introduction', in G. TEELING-SMITH (ed.), *Science, Industry and the State*. Oxford: Pergamon Press.

DURAND, C. (1962). 'Participation et Conflit: Orientations de la Recherche', Notes Critiques, *Sociologie du Travail*, IV, 1, Jan.–March: 64–74.

EARLEY, J. S. (1957). Critique of paper by H. A. Simon on 'Economics, Organization Theory, and Decision Making', *American Economic Review*, XLVII, 2, May: 330–5.

EASTWOOD, E. (1966). 'The Logic of Management', in *The Gentle Computer*, London: New Scientist.

Economists Advisory Group (1967). *The Economics of Advertising*, London: The Advertising Association.

ELLIOTT, O. (1960). *Men at the Top*, London: Weidenfeld & Nicolson.

EMERY, F. E. (1959). *Characteristics of Socio-Technical Systems*, London: Tavistock Institute of Human Relations, Doc. No. 527, mimeographed.

EMERY, F. E. and MAREK, J. (1962). 'Some Socio-Technical Aspects of Automation', *Human Relations*, 15: 17–25.

* EMERY, F. E. and TRIST, E. L. (1960). 'Socio-Technical Systems', in C. W. CHURCHMAN and M. VERHULST (eds.), *Management Sciences—Models and Techniques*, Vol. 2, London: Pergamon, 83–97. Explores the relationships in work organizations between technology, the structure of social relations and economic constraints.

* EMERY, F. E. and TRIST, E. L. (1965). 'The Causal Texture of Organizational Environments', *Human Relations*, 18, 1, Feb.: 21–32. Open-system analysis of interaction between an enterprise and its environment needs to be supplemented by an analysis of the inter-related processes in the environment itself.

ENGELS, F. (1845). *The Condition of the Working-Class in England*. Moscow: Foreign Languages Publishing House, 1953 edition.

ENNIS, R. W. (1967)—(ed.), *Accountability in Government Departments, Public Corporations and Public Companies*. London: Lyon, Grant & Green.

ETZIONI, A. (1960). 'Two Approaches to Organizational Analysis: A Critique and a Suggestion', *Administrative Science Quarterly*, 5, Sept.: 257–78.

European Economic Community (1966). *Basic Statistics of the Community*. Brussels: Statistical Office of the European Communities, 7th edition.

EVAN, W. M. (1962). 'Role Strain and the Norm of Reciprocity in Research Organizations', *American Journal of Sociology*, LXVIII, 3, Nov.: 346–54.

EVAN, W. M. (1965). 'Toward a Theory of Inter-Organizational Relations', *Management Science*, 11, 10, Aug.: 217–30.

EVELY, R. and LITTLE, I. M. D. (1960). *Concentration in British Industry*. Cambridge: The University Press.

FAUNCE, W. A. (1958). 'Automation in the Automobile Industry: Some Consequences for In-Plant Social Structure', *American Sociological Review*, 23: 401–7.

FAUNCE, W. A. (1959). 'Automation and Leisure', in H. B. JACOBSON and J. S. ROUCEK (eds.), *Automation and Society*. New York: Philosophical Library, Chapter 25.

* FAUNCE, W. A. (1968). *Problems of an Industrial Society*. New York: McGraw-Hill. Discusses characteristics of industrial societies and

considers problems relating to automation, alienation and individual freedom.

FAUNCE, W. A. and CLELLAND, D. A. (1963). 'The Professional Society', *New Society*, 7th Nov.: 14–16.

Federation of British Industries (1961). *Industrial Research in Manufacturing Industry 1959–60*. London: F.B.I.

* FELDMAN, A. S. and MOORE, W. E. (1965). 'Are Industrial Societies Becoming Alike?' in A. W. GOULDNER and S. M. MILLER (eds.), *Applied Sociology*. New York: Free Press. Stresses that there is 'no stable and enduring terminus to the industrialization process'.

FELLNER, W. (1949). *Competition Among the Few*. New York: Knopf.

FERGUSON, C. E. (1960). 'The Relationship of Business Size to Stability: An Empirical Approach', *Journal of Industrial Economics*, IX, 1, Nov.: 43–62.

FERRY, W. H. (1965), 'Irresponsibilities in Metrocorporate America', in A. HACKER (ed.), *The Corporation Take-Over*, New York: Doubleday, Chapter 6.

* FINER, S. E. (1956). 'The Political Power of Private Capital', *Sociological Review*, 3, 2; 279–94, and 4, 1: 5–30. Reviews methods used by firms in Britain to influence Government. Concludes that the power of private capital seems to be very effectively tempered by a respect for the rule of law.

FIRESTONE, O. J. (1967). *The Economic Implications of Advertising*. London: Methuen.

FLANDERS, A. (1964). *The Fawley Productivity Agreements*. London: Faber & Faber.

* FLANDERS, A. (1966). 'The Internal Social Responsibilities of Industry', *British Journal of Industrial Relations*, IV, 1, March: 1–21. Sees creative workplace bargaining as creating a new social relationship in industry in which it would be possible for the participants to act responsibly without abandoning their proper functions.

FLORENCE, P. S. (1961). *Ownership, Control and Success of Large Companies*. London: Sweet & Maxwell.

FLORENCE, P. S. (1962). *Post-War Investment, Location and Size of Plant*. Cambridge: The University Press for N.I.E.S.R.

FLORENCE, P. S. (1964). *Economics and Sociology of Industry*. London: Watts.

FORM, W. H. and GESCHWENDER, J. A. (1962). 'Social Reference Basis of Job Satisfaction: The Case of Manual Workers', *American Sociological Review*, 27, 2, April: 228–37.

FORM, W. H. and MILLER, D. C. (1960). *Industry, Labor and Community*. New York: Harper & Row.

FOSTER, D. (1963). 'What Sort of Automation?' *New Society*, 10th Oct.: 19–20.

* FOX, A. (1966). *Industrial Sociology and Industrial Relations*. Royal

Commission on Trade Unions and Employers' Associations, Research Paper no. 3, London: H.M.S.O. Contrasts two frames of reference for the analysis of industrial enterprise—as a unitary system and as a pluralistic system. Reviews a range of industrial sociological research.

FREEMAN, C. (1962). 'Research and Development: A Comparison Between British and American Industry', *National Institute Economic Review*, 20, May: 21–39.

FRENCH, J. R. P., ISRAEL, J. and ÅS, D. (1960). 'An Experiment on Participation in a Norwegian Factory', *Human Relations*, 13: 3–19.

FRENCH, J. R. P., KAHN, R. L. and MANN, F. C. (1962)—(eds.). Issue on 'Work, Health and Satisfaction', *Journal of Social Issues*, 18, 3.

FRIEDLANDER, F. (1965). 'Comparative Work Value Systems', *Personnel Psychology*, 18, 1, Spring: 1–20.

FRIEDLANDER, F. (1966). 'Importance of Work Versus Nonwork among Socially and Occupationally Stratified Groups', *Journal of Applied Psychology*, 50, 6, Dec.: 437–41.

FRIEDMAN, M. (1963). *Capitalism and Freedom*. Chicago: University of Chicago Press.

* FRIEDMANN, G. (1964). 'Tendances d'Aujourd'hui, Perspectives de Demain', in G. FRIEDMANN and P. NAVILLE (eds.), *Traité de Sociologie du Travail*. Paris: Librairie Colin, revised ed., vol. II: Chapter 25. Examines emerging trends with respect to the nature of work, occupational structure, organization, the problem of alienation, the importance of the non-work sphere, etc.

FRIEDMANN, W. G. (1957). 'Corporate Power, Government by Private Groups, and the Law', *Columbia Law Review*, LVII, Feb.: 155–86.

FROELICH, H. P. and WOLINS, L. (1960). 'Job Satisfaction as Need Satisfaction', *Personnel Psychology*, XIII: 407–20.

FRY, R. (1968). 'When a Discreet Institutional Nudge May Help', *The Times*, 18th Sept.: 24.

GALBRAITH, J. K. (1952). *American Capitalism: The Concept of Countervailing Power*. New York: Houghton Mifflin.

GALBRAITH, J. K. (1958). *The Affluent Society*. Harmondsworth: Penguin.

GALBRAITH, J. K. (1966). 1966 Reith Lectures on 'The New Industrial State', reported in *The Listener*, LXXVI, 17th Nov.–22nd Dec.

* GALBRAITH, J. K. (1967). *The New Industrial State*. London: Hamish Hamilton. Controversial analysis of modern American economic organization. Galbraith adopts a technologically deterministic view and thus predicts extensive convergence between advanced capitalist and communist systems.

GARDER, M. (1965). *L'Agonie du Régime en Russie Sovietique*, Paris: Dunoel.

GEORGE, K. D. (1967). 'Changes in British Industrial Concentration 1951–1958', *Journal of Industrial Economics*, 15, 3, July: 200–11.

GERTH, H. H. and MILLS, C. W. (1946). *From Max Weber: Essays in Sociology*. New York: Oxford University Press.

GERTH, H. H. and MILLS, C. W. (1952). 'A Marx for the Managers', in R. K.

MERTON, *et al.* (eds.), *Reader in Bureaucracy*, Glencoe, Ill.: Free Press: 165–78.

GILLESPIE, J. J. (1948). *Free Expression in Industry*. London: Pilot Press.

GLAZER, B. (1964). *Organizational Scientists, Their Professional Careers*, Indianapolis, Ind.: Bobbs-Merrill.

GOFFMAN, E. (1957). 'The Characteristics of Total Institutions', in Walter Reed Army Institute of Research, *Symposium on Preventive and Social Psychiatry*, Washington, D.C.: U.S. Government Printing Office: 43–84.

GOLDTHORPE, J. H. (1964). 'Social Stratification in Industrial Society', in P. HALMOS (ed.), *The Development of Industrial Societies*, Sociological Review Monograph No. 8: 97–122.

GOLDTHORPE, J. H. (1966a). 'Attitudes and Behaviour of Car Assembly Workers: A Deviant Case and a Theoretical Critique', *British Journal of Sociology*, XVII, 3, Sept.: 227–44.

GOLDTHORPE, J. H. (1966b). 'A Reply to Dunning and Hopper', *Sociological Review*, 14, 2, July: 187–95.

GOLDTHORPE, J. H. and LOCKWOOD, D. (1963). 'Affluence and the British Class Structure', *Sociological Review*, 11, 2, July: 133–63.

* GOLDTHORPE, J. H., LOCKWOOD, D., BECHHOFER, F. and PLATT, J. (1968). *The Affluent Worker: Industrial Attitudes and Behaviour*. Cambridge: The University Press. Study of 'affluent' workers in three plants at Luton, England. Concludes that worker attitudes and behaviour must in large part be explained in terms of their prior orientation to work and its social correlates.

GOODE, W. J. and FOWLER, I. (1949). 'Incentive Factors in a Low Morale Plant', *American Sociological Review*, 14, Oct., 619–24.

* GORDON, R. A. (1961). *Business Leadership in the Large Corporation*. Washington: Brookings Institution; 2nd edition by University of California Press with new Preface. Examined formal ownership and control position in 176 large US corporations in 1937–9. Attempted to move beyond reliance on purely mechanical criteria. Used published and interview data on 65 very large corporations to examine in which group business leadership was in practice located. Concluded that this was predominantly with 'professional executives'.

GOULDNER, A. W. (1955). 'Metaphysical Pathos and the Theory of Bureaucracy', *American Political Science Review*, XLIX: 496–507.

GRANICK, D. (1960). *The Red Executive*. New York: Doubleday.

GROSSFIELD, K. (1967). 'Government Support for Research and Development', *National Provincial Bank Review*, 77, Feb., 6–10.

GROVE, J. W. (1962). *Government and Industry in Britain*. London: Longmans.

Growth of Office Employment (1968). London: H.M.S.O.

GUEST, R. H. (1962). *Organizational Change*. Homewood, Ill.: Dorsey Press.

GUETZKOW, H. (1966). 'Relations among Organizations', in R. V. BOWERS (ed.), *Studies on Behavior in Organizations*, Athens: University of Georgia Press: 13–44.

134

GURIN, G., VEROFF, J. and FELD, S. (1960). *Americans View Their Mental Health*. New York: Basic Books.

GUTTSMAN, W. L. (1964). *The British Political Elite*. London: MacGibbon & Kee.

HACKER, A. (1965a). 'Introduction: Corporate America', in A. HACKER (ed.), *The Corporation Take-Over*. New York: Anchor Books 1-14.

* HACKER, A. (1965b). *The Corporation Take-Over*. New York: Anchor Books. A collection of papers which critically explore various aspects of the role of the business enterprise in a political democracy.

HAGE, J. and AIKEN, M. (1967). 'Program Change and Organizational Properties—A Comparative Analysis', *American Journal of Sociology*, 72, 5, March: 503-19.

* HAGE, J. and AIKEN, M. (1968). *Social Change in Complex Organization*, to be published by Rand McNally. Reviews research on correlates of social change in complex organizations, on the role of the environment in respect of organizational change, and on the process of such change.

* HAIRE, M., GHISELLI, E. E. and PORTER, L. W. (1966). *Managerial Thinking: An International Study*. New York: Wiley. Study of views on management held by over 3,600 managers from 14 countries. Found that about 25-30% of observed differences could be attributed consistently to managers' national origins.

HALL, D. T. and NOUGIAM, K. E. (1968). 'An Examination of Maslow's Need Hierarchy in an Organizational Setting', *Organizational Behaviour and Human Performance*, 3: 12-35.

HALL, R. H. (1968). 'Professionalization and Bureaucratization', *American Sociological Review*, 33, 1, Feb.: 92-104.

HALL, R. H., HAAS, J. E. and JOHNSON, N. J. (1967). 'Organizational Size, Complexity, and Formalization', *American Sociological Review*, 32, 6, Dec.: 903-12.

HALL, R. H. and TITTLE, C. R. (1966). 'A Note on Bureaucracy and its "Correlates" ', *American Journal of Sociology*, 72, 3, Nov.: 267-72.

HAMBERG, D. (1964). 'Size of Firm, Oligopoly and Research: The Evidence', *Canadian Journal of Economics and Political Science*, XXX, 1, Feb.: 62-75.

* HANDYSIDE, J. D. and SPEAK, M. (1964). 'Job satisfaction: Myths and Realities', *British Journal of Industrial Relations*, II, 1, March: 57-65. Reviews various studies by the NIIP. Stresses the multi-dimensional nature of job satisfaction.

Harvard Business Review (1961), 'How Ethical Are Businessmen?' July–Aug.: 6ff.

HARVEY, E. (1968). 'Technology and the Structure of Organizations', *American Sociological Review*, 33, 2: 247-59.

HAYEK, F. A. (1960). 'The Corporation in a Democratic Society', in M. ANSHEN and G. BACH (eds.), *Management and Corporations 1985*, New York: McGraw-Hill: 99-117.

HERZBERG, F., MAUSER, B., PETERSON, R. O. and CAPWELL, D. F. (1957). *Job*

Attitudes: Review of Research and Opinion, Pittsburgh: Psychological Services of Pittsburgh.

HICKSON, D. J. (1961). 'Motives of Workpeople who Restrict their Output', *Occupational Psychology,* 35, 3, July: 111–21.

HICKSON, D. J., PUGH, D. S. and PHEYSEY, D. C. (1969). 'Technology and Formal Organization: An Empirical Reappraisal', to appear in the *Administrative Science Quarterly.*

HININGS, C. R., PUGH, D. S. and HICKSON, D. J. (1969). 'The Ownership, Control and Decision-Making of Organizations', unpublished paper.

HODSON, R. (1967). 'Government and Industry: Learning to Co-exist', in A. ROBERTSON (ed.), *Penguin Survey of Business and Industry 1967,* Harmondsworth: Penguin: 17–27.

HOLTER, H. (1965). Attitudes Towards Employee Participation in Company Decision-making Processes', *Human Relations,* 18, 4, Nov.: 297–321.

HOMANS, G. C. (1951). *The Human Group.* London: Routledge & Kegan Paul.

HOOS, I. R. (1960). 'The Impact of Automation on Office Workers', *International Labour Review,* 82: 363–88.

HOOS, I. R. (1961). *Automation in the Office,* Washington, D. C.: Public Affairs Press.

HOPPER, E. (1965). 'Some Effects of Supervisory Style: A Sociological Analysis', *British Journal of Sociology,* XVI, 3, Sept.: 189–205.

House of Commons Parliamentary Debates, (Hansard), 8th July 1968, London: H.M.S.O.

HULIN, C. L. (1966). 'Effects of Community Characteristics on Measures of Job Satisfaction', *Journal of Applied Psychology,* 50, 2, April: 185–92.

* HULIN, C. L. and BLOOD, M. R. (1968). 'Job Enlargement, Individual Differences, and Worker Responses', *Psychological Bulletin,* 69, 1: 41–55. Concludes that employee reaction to job enlargement cannot be explained without reference to the degree to which employees accept or reject middle-class work-related values and norms.

INDIK, B. P. (1963). 'Some Effects of Organizational Size on Member Attitudes and Behaviour', *Human Relations,* 16: 369–84.

INDIK, B. P. (1965). 'Organization Size and Member Participation: Some Empirical Tests of Alternative Explanations', *Human Relations,* 18: 339–49.

* INGHAM, G. K. (1967). 'Organizational Size, Orientation to Work and Industrial Behaviour', *Sociology,* I, 3, Sept.: 239–58. Workers' orientations to work should be recognized as variables which intervene between organizational control structures (which tend to differ with size) and worker behaviour.

INGHAM, H. and HARRINGTON, L. T. (1958). *Interfirm Comparison for Management.* London: B.I.M.

JAHODA, M. (1958). *Positive Mental Health.* New York: Basic Books.

JAQUES, E. (1961). *Equitable Payment.* London: Heinemann.

JEWKES, J., SAWERS, D. and STILLERMAN, R. (1958). *The Sources of Invention*. London: Macmillan.

JOHNSON, E. C. (1967). 'Are the Mutual Funds too Powerful?' *The Times*, 16th May.

JOHNSON, R. (1966), letter to *The Guardian*, 27th Jan.

JONES, C. (1965). 'Government Relations with Science Based Industries', in G. TEELING-SMITH (ed.), *Science, Industry and the State*, Oxford: Pergamon: 71–80.

* JOSEPHSON, E. and JOSEPHSON, M. (1962)—(eds.), *Man Alone: Alienation in Modern Society*, New York: Dell. A useful collection of papers on the subject which does not draw exclusively on sociological contributions.

KARPIK, L. (1966). 'Urbanisation et Satisfactions au Travail', *Sociologie du Travail*, 8, 2: 179–204.

KATES, R. W. and WOHLWILL, J. F. (1966)—(eds.), 'Man's Response to the Physical Environment', *Journal of Social Issues*, XXII, 4, Oct.

* KATZ, D. and KAHN, R. L. (1966). *The Social Psychology of Organizations*. New York: Wiley. The most impressive of available contributions adopting a system approach to organizational analysis.

KATZELL, R. A., BARRETT, R. S. and PARKER, T. C. (1961). 'Job Satisfaction, Job Performance and Situational Characteristics', *Journal of Applied Psychology*, 45, 2, April: 65-72.

KAYSEN, C. (1957). 'The Social Significance of the Modern Corporation', *American Economic Review*, 47, May: 311–19.

KAYSEN, C. (1959). 'The Corporation: How Much Power? What Scope? in E. S. MASON (ed.), *The Corporation in Modern Society*, Cambridge, Mass.: Harvard University Press: Chapter 5.

* KERR, C., DUNLOP, J. T., HARBISON, F. H. and MYERS, C. A. (1960). *Industrialism and Industrial Man*. Cambridge, Mass.: Harvard University Press. Presents a theoretical statement on the 'logic' of industrialism, which hypothesises a convergent pattern of development.

KERR, C. and SIEGEL, A. (1954). 'The Interindustry Propensity to Strike— An International Comparison', in A. KORNHAUSER, R. DUBIN and A. M. ROSS (eds.), *Industrial Conflict*. New York: McGraw-Hill: 189–212.

KERSHAW, A. (1968). 'Galbraith Makes a Case for Advertising', *Advertising Quarterly*, 15, Spring: 9–16.

KNIGHT, R. (1967). 'Changes in the Occupational Structure of the Working Population', *Journal of the Royal Statistical Society*, 130, Part 3: 408–22.

KOLAJA, J. (1965). *Workers Councils: The Yugoslav Experience*. London: Tavistock.

KOLKO, G. (1962). *Wealth and Power in America*. New York: Praeger.

KORNHAUSER, A. (1962). 'Toward an Assessment of the Mental Health of Factory Workers: A Detroit Study', *Human Organizations*, 21, 1, Spring: 43–6.

KORNHAUSER, A. (1965). *Mental Health of the Industrial Worker—A Detroit Study*. New York: Wiley.

KORNHAUSER, W. (1962). *Scientists in Industry: Conflict and Accommodation*. Berkeley: University of California Press.

KREPS, T. J. (1962). 'Measurement of the Social Performance of Business', *The Annals of the American Academy of Political and Social Science*, 343, Sept. 20–31.

KRONSTEIN, H. (1965). 'Government and Business in International Trade', in A. HACKER (ed.), *The Corporation Take-Over*, New York: Anchor Books: Chapter 8.

LAMMERS, C. J. (1967). 'Power and Participation in Decision-Making in Formal Organizations', *American Journal of Sociology*, 73, 2, Sept.: 201–16.

LARNER, R. J. (1966). 'Ownership and Control in the 200 Largest Non-financial Corporations, 1929 and 1963', *American Economic Review*, LVI, 4, Sept.: 777–87.

LAVE, L. B. (1966). *Technological Change: Its Conception and Measurement*. Englewood Cliffs, N.J.: Prentice-Hall.

* LAWRENCE, P. R. and LORSCH, J. W. (1967). *Organization and Environment*. Boston: Harvard Graduate School of Business Administration, Division of Research. Data from ten business organizations in three industries indicate problems of combining differentiation with integration (conflict resolution) when coping with a rapidly changing environment.

LAZARSFELD, P. F. and OBERSCHALL, A. R. (1965). 'Max Weber and Empirical Social Research', *American Sociological Review*, 30, 2, April: 185–99.

LEAVITT, H. L. and WHISLER, T. L. (1958). 'Management in the 1980s', *Harvard Business Review*, 36, 6, Nov.–Dec.: 41–8.

Lectures on Economic Science (1870). Arranged by the National Association for the Promotion of Social Science, London: Longmans, Green.

LEE, J. (1921). *Management: A Study of Industrial Organisation*. London: Pitman.

LEVINE, S. and WHITE, P. E. (1961). 'Exchange as a Conceptual Framework for the Study of Interorganizational Relationships', *Administrative Science Quarterly*, 5: 583–601.

* LEVITT, T. (1958). 'The Dangers of Social Responsibility', *Harvard Business Review*, Sept.–Oct.: 41–50. Argues that primary business objectives should be efficiency and profitability. 'Welfare feudalism', lurking behind notions of business social responsibility, is a danger to individual liberty.

LEVY, M. J., JR. (1952). *The Structure of Society*. Princeton: Princeton University Press.

LEWIS, R. W. (1955). 'Measuring, Reporting and Appraising Results of Operations with Reference to Goals, Plans and Budgets', in *Planning, Managing and Measuring the Business: A Case Study of Management planning and Control at General Electric Company*. New York: Controllership Foundation: Part V: 29–41.

LIKERT, R. (1961). *New Patterns of Management.* New York: McGraw-Hill.

LIKERT, R. (1963). 'Trends Toward a World-Wide Theory of Management,' in *Proceedings of CIOS XIII International Management Congress,* 2: 110–14.

LIKERT, R. (1967). *The Human Organization: Its Management and Value.* New York: McGraw-Hill.

LINTNER, J. (1956). 'Distribution of Incomes of Corporations among Dividends, Retained Earnings, and Taxes', *American Economic Review,* XLVI, 2, May: 97–113.

LINTNER, J. (1959). 'The Financing of Corporations', in E. S. MASON (ed.), *The Corporation in Modern Society.* Cambridge, Mass.: Harvard University Press: Chapter 9.

LIPSET, S. M. (1963). *Political Man.* London: Mercury Books.

LIPSET, S. M., TROW, M. A. and COLEMAN, J. S. (1956). *Union Democracy.* Glencoe, Ill.: Free Press.

LIPSEY, R. G. (1966). *An Introduction to Positive Economics.* London: Weidenfeld & Nicolson.

LITTLE, I. M. D. (1957). *A Critique of Welfare Economics.* London: Oxford University Press. 2nd edition.

LITWAK, E. and HYLTON, L. F. (1962). 'Interorganizational Analysis: A Hypothesis on Co-ordinating Agencies', *Administrative Science Quarterly,* 6: 395–420.

LOCKWOOD, D. (1964). A Comment on 'The Distribution of Power in Industrial Society', in P. HALMOS (ed.), *The Development of Industrial Societies,* Sociological Review Monograph No. 8, Oct.: 35–41.

* LOMAX, K. S. (1965). *The Assessment of Economic Performance.* Leeds: University Press. On problems involved in the accountant's and the statistician's approaches to assessing economic performance.

LONG, N. E. (1959). 'The Corporation, its Satellites, and the Local Community', in E. S. MASON (ed.), *The Corporation in Modern Society,* Cambridge, Mass.: Harvard University Press: Chapter 10.

LUPTON, T. (1963). *On the Shop Floor.* Oxford: Pergamon.

* LUPTON, T. and WILSON, S. (1959). 'The Social Background and Connections of Top Decision Makers', *Manchester School of Economics and Social Studies,* Jan.: 30–51. Uses evidence presented to the Parker Tribunal to trace kinship relations and other social connections between persons prominent in British banking, insurance, politics, and public administration.

LYMAN, E. L. (1955). 'Occupational Differences in the Value Attached to Work', *American Journal of Sociology,* LXI, 2, Sept.: 138–44.

MCCLELLAND, W. G. (1966). *Costs and Competition in Retailing.* London: Macmillan.

MCGREGOR, D. (1960). *The Human Side of Enterprise.* New York: McGraw-Hill.

MACLAURIN, W. R. (1954). 'Technological Progress in Some American Industries', *American Economic Review,* Papers and Proceedings, May: 178–189.

MANN, F. C. (1962). 'Psychological and Organizational Impacts', in J. T. DUNLOP (ed.), *Automation and Technological Change.* Englewood

Cliffs, N. J.: Prentice-Hall: 43–65.

MANN, F. C. and HOFFMAN, L. R. (1960). *Man and Automation*. New York: Holt.

MANSFIELD, E. (1963a). 'Size of Firm, Market Structure and Innovation', *Journal of Political Economy*, 71, 6, Dec.: 556–76.

MANSFIELD, E. (1963b). 'The Speed of Response of Firms to New Techniques', *Quarterly Journal of Economics*, LXXVII, 2, May: 290–311.

MANSFIELD, E. (1964a)—(ed.), *Monopoly Power and Economic Performance*. New York: Norton.

MANSFIELD, E. (1964b). 'Industrial Research and Development Expenditures–Determinants, Prospects, and Relation to Size of Firm and Inventive Output', *Journal of Political Economy*, LXXII, Aug.: 319–40.

* MARCH, J. G. (1965)—(ed.), *Handbook of Organizations*. Chicago: Rand McNally. An extensive compendium of available knowledge on organizational behaviour. Amply referenced.

* MARCH, J. G. and SIMON, H. A. (1958). *Organizations*. New York: Wiley. Systematically presents numerous propositions on organizations within a framework which stresses individual decision-making. Ten years ahead of its time.

MARCSON, S. (1960). *The Scientist in American Industry*. Princeton: University of Princeton Press.

* MARCUSE, H. (1964). *One Dimensional Man: The Ideology of Industrial Society*. London: Routledge & Kegan Paul. Individual freedom is limited by the benign bureaucracy of modern technological societies, capitalist and communist. Instructive to compare with Galbraith (1967).

MARRIS, R. L. (1964). *The Economic Theory of 'Managerial' Capitalism*. London: Macmillan.

MARRIS, R. L. (1967). 'Profitability and Growth in the Individual Firm', *Business Ratios*, 1, Spring: 3–12.

MARROW, A. J., BOWERS, D. G. and SEASHORE, S. E. (1967). *Management by Participation: Creating a Climate for Personal and Organizational Development*. New York: Harper & Row.

MARSHALL, A. (1919). *Industry and Trade*. London: Macmillan.

MARX, K. and ENGELS, F. (1848). *Manifesto of the Communist Party*, first publ. London 1848, transl. by Foreign Languages Publishing House, Moscow 1959.

MARX, K. (1844). *Economic and Philosophical Manuscripts of 1844*. Moscow: Foreign Languages Publishing House 1959.

MASLOW, A. H. (1943). 'A Theory of Human Motivation', *Psychological Review*, 50: 370–96.

MASLOW, A. H. (1954). *Motivation and Personality*. New York: Harper.

MASON, E. S. (1958). 'The Apologetics of "Managerialism"', *The Journal of Business*, XXXI, 1, Jan.: 1–11.

* MASON, E. S. (1959)—(ed.), *The Corporation in Modern Society*. Cambridge, Mass.: Harvard University Press. A collection of essays which explore many key issues.

MAXCY, G. and SILBERSTON, A. (1959). *The Motor Industry*. London: Allen & Unwin.

MAYO, E. (1933). *The Human Problems of an Industrial Civilization*. New York: Macmillan.

MAYO, E. (1945). *The Social Problems of an Industrial Civilization*. Boston, Mass.: Harvard University Press.

MEADE, J. E. (1968). 'Is "The New Industrial State" Inevitable?' *Economic Journal*, LXXVIII, 310, June: 372–92.

MEANS, G. C. (1931). 'The Growth in the Relative Importance of the Large Corporation in American Economic Life', *American Economic Review*, XXI: 10–42.

MELMAN, S. (1958). *Decision Making and Productivity*. Oxford: Blackwell.

MERTON, R. K., GRAY, A. P., HOCKEY, B. and SELVIN, H. C. (1952)—(eds.), *Reader in Bureaucracy*. New York: Free Press.

MERTON, R. K. (1957). *Social Theory and Social Structure*. Glencoe, Ill.: Free Press.

MICHELS, R. (1915). *Political Parties*. New York: Collier Books (1962 edition).

MILIBAND, R. (1968). 'Professor Galbraith and American Capitalism', *The Socialist Register 1968*, London: Merlin Press: 215–29.

* MILLER, D. C. and FORM, W. H. (1964). *Industrial Sociology: The Sociology of Work Organizations*. New York: Harper & Row. 2nd edition. A standard text, largely confined to American sources.

MILLER, E. J. and RICE, A. K. (1967). *Systems of Organization: The Control of Task and Sentient Boundaries*. London: Tavistock.

MILLER, G. A. (1967). 'Professionals in Bureaucracy: Alienation Among Industrial Scientists and Engineers', *American Sociological Review*, 32, 5, Oct.: 755–68.

MILLER, M. (1965). *Rise of the Russian Consumer*. London: Institute of Economic Affairs.

MILLS, C. W. (1956). *The Power Elite*. New York: Oxford University Press.

MILLS, C. W. (1963). *The Marxists*. Harmondsworth: Penguin.

MILLWARD, N. (1968). 'Family Status and Behaviour at Work', *Sociological Review*, 16, 2, July: 149–64.

* MOORE, W. E. (1962). *The Conduct of the Corporation*. New York: Random House. A witty 'guided tour' through the business corporation. A strictly personal peep through many keyholes.

MOORE, W. E. (1965). *The Impact of Industry*. Englewood Cliffs, N. J.: Prentice-Hall.

MOOS, S. (1964). 'Automation: A Worker's Balance Sheet', *New Society*, 6th Aug.: 19–20.

MORSE, N. C. (1953). *Satisfactions in the White-Collar Job*. Ann Arbor: University of Michigan.

MORSE, N. C. and REIMER, E. (1956). 'The Experimental Change of a

Major Organizational Variable', *Journal of Abnormal and Social Psychology*, 52, Jan.: 120–29.

MOTT, P. E., MANN, F. C., MCLOUGHLIN, Q. and WARWICK, D. P. (1965). *Shift Work: The Social, Psychological and Physical Consequences*. Ann Arbor: University of Michigan Press.

MUELLER, D. C. (1966). 'Patents, Research and Development and the Measurement of Inventive Activity', *Journal of Industrial Economics*, XV, 1, Nov.: 26–37.

MUKERJI, G. P. (1963). 'On Size-Productivity Relationship in Indian Industries', *Journal of Industrial Economics*, XI, 2, April: 141–59.

MUMFORD, E. and BANKS, O. (1967). *The Computer and the Clerk*. London: Routledge & Kegan Paul.

MUMFORD, E. and WARD, T. (1965). 'How the Computer Changes Management', *New Society*, 23rd Sept.: 6–10.

MYRDAL, G. (1963). *Challenge to Affluence*. New York: Pantheon.

* NATH, R. (1968). 'A Methodological Review of Cross-Cultural Management Research', *International Social Science Journal*, XX, 1: 35–62. A valuable review, with an extensive bibliography.

NAVILLE, P. (1961). *L'Automation et le Travail Humain*. Paris: CNRS.

NAVILLE, P. (1963). *Vers l' Automatisme Social? Problèmes du Travail et de l'Automation*. Paris: Gallimard.

NAVILLE, P. and PALIERNE, J. (1960). 'Automation et Travail Humain: le Cas de la "Télétypesetter" ', *Sociologie du Travail*, 2, 3, July/Sept.: 193–205.

NEAL, A. G. and RETTIG, S. (1967). 'On the Multidimensionality of Alienation', *American Sociological Review*, 32, 1, Feb.: 54–64.

NEALE, A. D. (1966). *The Anti-Trust Laws of the United States of America*. Cambridge: The University Press.

NEHNEVAJSA, J. (1959). 'Automation and Social Stratification', in H. B. JACOBSON and J. S. ROUCEK (eds.), *Automation and Society*, New York: Philosophical Library: Chapter 31.

NEULOH, O. (1966). 'A New Definition of Work and Leisure under Advanced Technology', in J. STIEBER (ed.), *Employment Problems of Automation and Advanced Technology*, London: Macmillan: 200–12.

NEWTON, K. (1968). *The Sociology of British Communism*. London: Allen Lane The Penguin Press.

* NICHOLS, W. A. T. (1967). *Ownership, Control and Ideology: An Enquiry Into Certain Aspects of Modern Business Ideology*. Unpublished Master's thesis, University of Hull (to be published by Allen & Unwin, London). An excellent review of the debate and evidence on ownership, control and the ideology of top managers. Presents results of the author's own research into values of senior British executives.

NICHOLSON, R. J. (1967). 'The Distribution of Personal Income', *Lloyds Bank Review*, 83, Jan.: 11–21.

NOVE, A. (1968a). 'Economic Policy and Economic Trends', in A. DALLIN and T. B. LARSON (eds.), *Soviet Politics Since Khruschev*, Englewood Cliffs, N. J.: Prentice-Hall: Chapter 4.

NOVE, A. (1968b). 'Resistance to Reforms', *The Times*, Supplement on 'The Soviet Union', 21st June.

* NOVE, A. (1969). *The Soviet Economy*. London: Allen & Unwin. 3rd edition. A further up-dating of a standard text.

NOWOTNY, O. H. (1964). 'American Versus European Management Philosophy', *Harvard Business Review*, 42, 2, March–April: 101–8.

ORTH, C. D., BAILEY, J. C. and WOLEK, F. W. (1965). *Administering Research and Development*. London: Tavistock.

OXENFELDT, A. R. (1963)—(ed.), *Models of Markets*. New York: Columbia University Press.

PACKARD, V. (1961). *The Waste Makers*. London: Longmans.

PAINE, F. T., DEUTSCH, D. R. and SMITH, R. A. (1967). 'Relationships between Family Backgrounds and Work Values', *Journal of Applied Psychology*, 51, 4, Aug.: 320–3.

PARKER, S. R. (1964). *Work Satisfaction: A Review of the Literature*. London: Government Social Survey Methodological Paper No. 115, Dec., mimeographed.

PARKER, S. R. (1965). 'Work and Non-Work in Three Occupations', *Sociological Review*, 13, March: 65–75.

* PARKER, S. R., BROWN, R. K., CHILD, J. and SMITH, M. A. (1968). *The Sociology of Industry*. London: Allen & Unwin. Concise review of issues, research and sources which gives particular attention to British work where possible.

PARRY, A. (1966). *The New Class Divided: Science and Technology Versus Communism*. New York: Macmillan.

PARSONS, T. (1952). *The Social System*. London: Tavistock.

PARSONS, T. (1956). 'Suggestions for a Sociological Approach to the Theory of Organizations, I and II', *Administrative Science Quarterly*, 1, June and Sept.: 63–85: 225–39.

* PARSONS, T. and SMELSER, N. J. (1957). *Economy and Society*. London: Routledge & Kegan Paul. Functionalist model exploring the role of the enterprise and the economy within the wider society. Utilizes concept of 'boundary interchange' to indicate functional interactions between economic and other social systems.

PAYNE, R. L. and HICKSON, D. J. (1967). 'Measuring the Ghost in the Organizational Machine', *European Business*, 13, May: 41–5.

PAYNE, R. L. (1968). *Factor Analysis of a Maslow-Type Need Satisfaction Questionnaire*. Industrial Administration Research Unit, University of Aston in Birmingham, mimeographed.

PEARLIN, L. I. (1962). 'Alienation from Work: A Study of Nursing Personnel', *American Sociological Review*, 27: 314–26.

PELZ, D. C. (1952). 'Influence: A Key to Effective Leadership in the First-Line Supervisor', *Personnel*, 29, Nov.: 209–17.

PENROSE, E. T. (1959). *The Theory of the Growth of the Firm*. Oxford: Blackwell.

P.E.P. (1957). *Three Case Studies in Automation.* London: P.E.P.

PERROW, C. (1961). 'The Analysis of Goals in Complex Organizations', *American Sociological Review*, 26, 6, Dec.: 854–66.

PERROW, C. (1967). 'A Framework for the Comparative Analysis of Organizations', *American Sociological Review*, 32, 2, April: 194–208.

PETERSON, R. B. (1968). 'The Swedish Experience with Industrial Democracy', *British Journal of Industrial Relations*, VI, 2, July: 185–203.

PETIT, T. A. (1967). *The Moral Crisis in Management.* New York: McGraw-Hill.

PLATT, J. A. (1964). 'Social Stratification in Industrial Society: A Comment', in *The Development of Industrial Societies*, Sociological Review Monograph No. 8, University of Keele: 133–40.

POLLARD, S. (1965). *The Genesis of Modern Management.* London: Edward Arnold.

POLLOCK, F. (1957). *Automation: Its Economic and Social Consequences.* New York: Praeger. (Translation of *Automation: Materialien zur Beurteilung ihrer Ökonomischen und Sozialen Folgen*, Frankfurt: Europäische Verlagsanstalt.)

POPE LEO XIII (1891). *Rerum Novarum:* 'Of the Condition of the Working Classes', Rome, 15th May.

POPPER, K. R. (1957). *The Poverty of Historicism.* London: Routledge & Kegan Paul.

PORTER, L. W. (1962–4). 'Job Attitudes in Management I–VI', *Journal of Applied Psychology*, 46, 1962: 375–84; 47, 1963: 141–8, 267–75, 386–97; 48, 1964: 31–6, 305–9.

* PORTER, L. W. and LAWLER, E. E. (1965). 'Properties of Organization Structure in Relation to Job Attitudes and Job Behaviour', *Psychological Bulletin*, 64: 23–51. Reviews results of empirical field studies on the relationships between seven structural properties of organizations and job attitudes and behaviour in business or industrial organizations.

PRATTEN, C. and DEAN, R. M., in collaboration with A. SILBERSTON (1965). *The Economies of Large-Scale Production in British Industry.* Cambridge: The University Press.

PREST, A. R. and STARK, T. (1967). 'Some Aspects of Income Distribution in the U.K. since World War II', *Manchester School of Social and Economic Studies*, Sept.: 217–43.

PUGH, D. S. (1966). 'Modern Organization Theory: A Psychological and Sociological Study', *Psychological Bulletin*, 66, 4: 235–51.

PUGH, D. S., HICKSON, D. J., HININGS, C. R., MACDONALD, K. M., TURNER, C. and LUPTON, T. (1963). 'A Conceptual Scheme for Organizational Analysis', *Administrative Science Quarterly*, 8, 3, Dec.: 289–315.

PUGH, D. S., HICKSON, D. J., HININGS, C. R. and TURNER, C. (1969). 'The Context of Organization Structures', *Administrative Science Quarterly*, to appear.

RAY, G. F. (1966). 'The Size of Plant: A Comparison', *National Institute Economic Review*, 38, Nov.: 63–6.

RENOLD, C. G. (1950). *Joint Consultation Over Thirty Years*. London: Allen & Unwin.

REVANS, R. W. (1958). 'Human Relations, Management and Size', in E. M. HUGH-JONES (ed.), *Human Relations and Modern Management*. Amsterdam: Nth. Holland Pub. Co.: Chapter 7.

REVANS, R. W. (1960). 'Industrial Morale and Size of Unit', in W. GALENSON and S. M. LIPSET (eds.), *Labor and Trade Unionism*. New York: Wiley: 259–300.

REVELL, J. and MOYLE, J. (1966). *The Owners of Quoted Ordinary Shares: A Survey for 1963*. London: Chapman & Hall.

RHEE, H. A. (1968). *Office Automation in Social Perspective*. Oxford: Blackwell.

RICE, A. K. (1958). *Productivity and Social Organization: The Ahmedabad Experiment*. London: Tavistock.

* RICE, A. K. (1963). *The Enterprise and its Environment: A System Theory of Management*. London: Tavistock. Continues Rice's earlier review of directed experiments in the Indian textile industry. Placed in an open-system analytical framework.

RICHARDSON, S. A. (1956). 'Organizational Contrasts on British and American Ships', *Administrative Science Quarterly*, I, 2, Sept.: 189–207.

* RICHMAN, B. M. (1965). *Soviet Management*. Englewood Cliffs, N. J.: Prentice-Hall. Utilizes data from personal interviews in 1960–1 in addition to published sources. Updates previous major sources such as Berliner (1957) and Granick (1960).

RICHMAN, B. M. (1967). *Management Development and Education in the Soviet Union*. Michigan: M.S.U. International Business Studies.

RIDDELL, D. S. (1968). 'Social Self-Government: The Background of Theory and Practice in Yugoslav Socialism', *British Journal of Sociology*, XIX, 1, March: 47–75.

RIESMAN, D. (1953). *Thorstein Veblen: A Critical Interpretation*. New York: Scribners.

RIMLINGER, G. V. (1959). 'International Differences in the Strike Propensity of Coal Miners: Experience in Four Countries', *Industrial and Labor Relations Review*, 12, 3, April: 389–405.

ROBINSON, E. A. G. (1953). *The Structure of Competitive Industry*. London: Nisbet.

ROETHLISBERGER, F. J. and DICKSON, W. J. (1939). *Management and the Worker*. Cambridge, Mass.: Harvard University Press.

ROGOW, A. A. and SHORE, P. (1955). *The Labour Government and British Industry*. Oxford: Blackwell.

ROSE, A. M. (1967). 'Confidence and the Corporation', *American Journal of Economics & Sociology*, 26, 3, July: 231–6.

ROSE, J. (1967). *Automation: Its Uses and Consequences*. London: Oliver & Boyd.

ROSS, A. M. and HARTMAN, P. T. (1960). *Changing Patterns of Industrial Conflict.* New York: Wiley.

ROSS, A. M. and IRWIN, D. (1951). 'Strike Experience in Five Countries 1927–1947: An Interpretation', *Industrial and Labor Relations Review*, 4, 3, April: 323–42.

ROSTOW, E. V. (1959). 'To Whom and for What Ends Is Corporate Management Responsible?' in E. S. MASON (ed.), *The Corporation in Modern Society.* Cambridge, Mass.: Harvard University Press, Chapter 3.

ROY, D. F. (1952). 'Quota Restriction and Goldbricking in a Machine Shop', *American Journal of Sociology*, 57, 5, March: 427–42.

RUSHING, W. A. (1966). 'Organizational Size, Rules and Surveillance', *Journal of Experimental Social Psychology*, 2, 1, Feb.: 11–26.

* SADLER, P. (1968). *Social Research on Automation.* London: Heinemann (for SSRC). A handy easy-to-read map of the field, providing a brief review of major issues, problems, progress and sources.

SAMUEL, R. (1960). ' "Bastard" Capitalism', in *Out of Apathy.* London: Stevens: 19–55.

SAMUELS, J. M. and SMYTH, D. J. (1968). 'Profits, Variability of Profits and Firm Size', *Economica*, XXXV, 138, May: 127–39.

SAYLES, L. R. (1958). *Behavior of Industrial Work Groups: Prediction and Control.* New York: Wiley.

SCHAFFER, R. H. (1953). 'Job Satisfaction as Related to Need Satisfaction in Work', *Psychological Monographs*, Vol. 67, Pt. 14, No. 364, *passim.*

SCHEIN, E. H. (1965). *Organizational Psychology.* Englewood Cliffs, N.J.: Prentice-Hall.

SCHEIN, E. H. and OTT, J. S. (1962). 'The Legitimacy of Organizational Influence', *American Journal of Sociology*, 67, May: 682–9.

SCHERER, F. M. (1965). 'Firm Size, Market Structure, Opportunity, and the Output of Patented Inventions', *American Economic Review*, LV, 5: 1097–1125.

* SCHNEIDER, E. V. (1957). *Industrial Sociology: The Social Relations of Industry and the Community.* New York: McGraw-Hill. Though dated, this is probably still the most sophisticated American text available in its field.

SCHUMPETER, J. A. (1942). *Capitalism, Socialism, and Democracy.* New York: Harper.

SCHWARTZMAN, D. (1963). 'Uncertainty and the Size of the Firm', *Economica*, Aug.: 287–96.

SCOTT, W. H. (1965). *Office Automation: Administrative and Human Problems.* Paris: O.E.C.D.

* SEEMAN, M. (1959). 'On the Meaning of Alienation', *American Sociological Review*, 24, Dec.: 783–91. An influential paper which attempts to classify five main dimensions of alienation at the subjective level.

SHANKS, M. (1967). *The Innovators: The Economics of Technology.* Harmondsworth: Penguin.

SHELDON, O. (1923). *The Philosophy of Management*. London: Pitman.

SHEPHERD, C. (1961). 'Orientations of Scientists and Engineers', *Pacific Sociological Review*, 4, Fall: 79–83.

SHEPHERD, W. G. (1964). 'Trends of Concentration in American Manufacturing Industries, 1947–1958', *Review of Economics and Statistics*, XLVI, 2, May: 200–12.

SHEPHERD, W. G. (1966). 'Changes in British Industrial Concentration 1951–1958', *Oxford Economic Papers*, 18, 1, March: 126–32.

SHIMMIN, S. (1962). 'Extra-Mural Factors Influencing Behaviour at Work', *Occupational Psychology*, 36, 3, July: 124–31.

* SHONFIELD, A. (1965). *Modern Capitalism: The Changing Balance of Public and Private Power*. London: Oxford University Press. Traces the distinctive features and developments of post-war capitalism, which include a conscious pursuit of full employment, accelerated technical progress and increasing governmental economic regulation. Yet substantial inter-societal differences remain.

SIEGEL, A. J. (1957). 'The Economic Environment in Human Relations Research', in C. M. ARENSBERG et al. (eds.), *Research in Industrial Human Relations*. New York: Harper: Chapter 6.

SIGAL, C. (1960). *Weekend in Dinlock*. London: Secker & Warburg.

* SILVERMAN, D. (1968a). 'Formal Organizations or Industrial Sociology: Towards a Social Action Analysis of Organizations', *Sociology*, 2, 2, May: 221–38. Argues for renewed attention to be given to industrial sociology in order to counter-balance the recent emphasis on formal organization theory. The social action perspective on organizational behaviour is presented as an alternative to the structural-functionalism contained in much organization theory.

SILVERMAN, D. (1968b). Book Review in the *British Journal of Industrial Relations*, VI, 3, Nov.: 393–7.

SIMON, H. A. (1947). *Administrative Behavior*. New York: Macmillan.

SIMON, H. A. (1965). *The Shape of Automation for Men and Management*. New York: Harper.

SINGLETON, F. and TOPHAM, A. (1963). *Workers' Control in Yugoslavia*. London: Fabian Research Series, No. 233.

SJOBERG, G. (1964). 'Community', in J. GOULD and W. L. KOLB (eds.), *A Dictionary of the Social Sciences*. New York: Free Press: 114–15.

SLOAN, A. P., JR. (1965). *My Years With General Motors*. London: Sidgwick & Jackson.

SMIGEL, E. O. (1963)—(ed.), *Work and Leisure: A Contemporary Social Problem*. New Haven, Conn.: College & University Press.

SMITH, M. A. (1968). 'Process Technology and Powerlessness', *British Journal of Sociology*, XIX, 1, March: 76–88.

SMITH, R. A. (1963). *Corporations in Crisis*. New York: Doubleday.

STACEY, N. A. H. (1966). *Mergers in Modern Business*. London: Hutchinson.

STETTNER, L. (1966). 'Survey of Literature on Social and Economic Effects of Technological Change', in J. STIEBER (ed.), *Employment Problems of Automation and Advanced Technology*. London: Macmillan: 451–79.

* STIEBER, J. (1966)—(ed.), *Employment Problems of Automation and Advanced Technology*. London: Macmillan. Collected papers of a high standard covering progress of advanced technology, its implications for education and training, and its impact on employment, management, and industrial relations.

STRACHEY, J. (1956). *Contemporary Capitalism*. London: Gollancz.

STRAUSS, G. (1963a). 'Some Notes on Power-Equalization', in H. J. LEAVITT (ed.), *The Social Science of Organizations*. Englewood Cliffs, N. J.: Prentice-Hall: 39–84.

STRAUSS, G. (1963b). 'The Personality-Versus-Organization Theory', in L. R. SAYLES (ed.), *Individualism and Big Business*. New York: McGraw-Hill: 67–80.

STURMTHAL, A. (1964). *Workers' Councils: A Study of Workplace Organization on Both Sides of the Iron Curtain*. Cambridge, Mass.: Harvard University Press.

TALACCHI, S. (1960). 'Organization Size, Individual Attitudes and Behavior: An Empirical Study', *Administrative Science Quarterly*, 5: 398–420.

TATU, M. (1965). 'Russia's New Class', *New Society*, 7th Oct.: 15–17.

TAWNEY, R. H. (1921). *The Acquisitive Society*. London: Bell. (Fontana Books edition, London, 1961.)

TELSER, L. G. (1965). *Advertising and Competition*, London: Institute of Economic Affairs.

TERREBERRY, S. (1968). 'The Evolution of Organizational Environments', *Administrative Science Quarterly*, 12, 4, March: 590–613.

The Annals of the American Academy of Political and Social Science (1962), Special Issue on 'The Ethics of Business Enterprise', 343, Sept.

The Economist, 14th Jan. 1967, 'Bigness in Industry: Not Always Best': 136–7.

The Observer, 16th June 1968, 'Taxpayers' Takeover': 11.

The Redundancy Payments Act 1965.

The Times, 28th May 1962, 'Voteless Shares Again Come Under Fire'.

The Times, 9th Feb. 1968, 'Britain's Banking Revolution'.

The Times, 17th July 1968, Financial Editor, 'Panel Should Probe Buying of Gallaher'.

The Times, 27th July 1968, Leader, The Times Business News, 'Safeguarding the Shareholders' Interest'.

The Times, 29th July 1968, (a) 'Say in Industry for Workers Urged'. (b) 'Limits to Sharing' (1st Leader).

The Times 500 (1968), 'Leading Companies in Britain and Overseas 1968–69', London: Times Newspapers Ltd.

THOMPSON, J. D. (1967). *Organizations in Action*. New York: McGraw-Hill.

THOMPSON, J. D. and MCEWEN, W. J. (1958). 'Organizational Goals and

Environment: Goal-Setting as an Interaction Process', *American Sociological Review*, 23, Feb.: 23–31.

TIVEY, L. (1966). *Nationalization in British Industry*. London: Cape.

TRIST, E. L. and BAMFORTH, K. W. (1951). 'Some Social and Psychological Consequences of the Longwall Method of Coal Getting', *Human Relations*, IV, Feb.: 3–38.

* TRIST, E. L., HIGGIN, G. W., MURRAY, H. and POLLOCK, A. B. (1963). *Organizational Choice*. London: Tavistock. Studies of coal-mining in Britain which indicate that alternative forms of work organization possessing different consequences for productivity and morale may be available within the same technological limits.

TUGENDHAT, C. (1968a). 'How the International Giants Affect World Trading Patterns', *Financial Times*, 18th Dec.

TUGENDHAT, C. (1968b). 'Gigantomania', *Financial Times*, 7th Dec.

TURNER, A. N. and LAWRENCE, P. R. (1965). *Industrial Jobs and the Worker —An Investigation of Response to Task Attributes*. Boston, Mass.: Division of Research, Harvard Business School.

UDY, S. H., JR. (1959). *The Organization of Work*. New Haven: HRAF Press.

United Nations (1965). *Statistical Yearbook for 1964*. New York: U.N.O.

United Nations (1967). *Statistical Yearbook for 1966*. New York: U.N.O.

URWICK, L. and BRECH, E. F. L. (1947). *The Making of Scientific Management*, Vol. II, 'Management in British Industry'. London: Pitman.

VATTER, H. G. (1964). 'Market', in J. GOULD and W. L. KOLB (eds.), *A Dictionary of the Social Sciences*. New York: Free Press: 407–9.

VEBLEN, T. (1899). *The Theory of the Leisure Class*. New York: Macmillan.

VEBLEN, T. (1904). *The Theory of Business Enterprise*. New York: Scribners.

VEBLEN, T. (1914). *The Instinct of Workmanship*. New York: Macmillan.

VEBLEN, T. (1921). *The Engineers and the Price System*. New York: Viking.

VEBLEN, T. (1923). *Absentee Ownership and Business Enterprise in Recent Times: The Case of America*. London: Allen & Unwin.

VERNON, R. (1959). 'The American Corporation in Underdeveloped Areas', in E. S. MASON (ed.), *The Corporation in Modern Society*. Cambridge, Mass.: Harvard University Press: Chapter 12.

* VILLAREJO, D. (1961–2). 'Stock Ownership and the Control of Corporations', *New University Thought*. Chicago, Autumn 1961: 33–77; Winter, 1962: 47–65. Detailed analysis of stockholdings of directors in the 250 largest American industrial firms. Concluded that in at least 141 of these firms concentrated ownership among directors was sufficient to secure potential operating control.

VROOM, V. H. (1959). 'Some Personality Determinants of the Effects of Participation', *Journal of Abnormal and Social Psychology*, 59: 322–7.

VROOM, V. H. (1960). *Some Personality Determinants of the Effects of Participation*. Englewood Cliffs, N. J.: Prentice-Hall.

* VROOM, V. H. (1964). *Work and Motivation*. New York: Wiley. Excellent review of research on the motivational determinants of occupational choice, work satisfaction and job performance.

WALKER, C. R. and GUEST, R. H. (1952). *The Man on the Assembly Line*. Cambridge, Mass.: Harvard University Press.

WALPOLE, G. S. (1944). *Management and Men: A Study of the Theory and Practice of Joint Consultation at all Levels*. London: Cape.

* WALTON, C. C. (1967). *Corporate Social Responsibilities*. Belmont, Calif.: Wadsworth. Classifies and sets out the conflicting views on the question of business social responsibility.

WARNER, W. K. and HILANDER, J. S. (1964). 'The Relationship between Size of Organization and Membership Participation', *Rural Sociology*, 29, 1, March: 30–9.

WARNER, W. L. and ABEGGLEN, J. C. (1955). *Big Business Leaders in America*. New York: Harper.

WARNER, W. L., UNWALLA, D. B. and TRIMM, J. H. (1967). *The Emergent American Society*, Vol. I, 'Large Scale Organizations'. New Haven, Conn.: Yale University Press.

WASSERMAN, P. (1959). *Measurement and Evaluation of Organizational Performance: An Annotated Bibliography*. Ithaca, N.Y.: Cornell University.

WEBB, B. and WEBB, S. (1897). *Industrial Democracy*. London: Longmans, Green.

WEBER, M. (1930). *The Protestant Ethic and the Spirit of Capitalism*. London: Allen & Unwin.

WEBER, M. (1947). *The Theory of Social and Economic Organization* (transl. A. M. HENDERSON and T. PARSONS). New York: Oxford University Press.

WEDDERBURN, K. W. (1965). *The Worker and the Law*. Harmondsworth: Penguin.

WESTERGAARD, J. H. (1965). 'The Withering Away of Class: A Contemporary Myth', in P. ANDERSON and R. BLACKBURN (eds.), *Towards Socialism*. London: Fontana: 77–113.

WHISLER, T. L. (1966). 'The Impact of Advanced Technology on Managerial Decision-Making', in J. STIEBER (ed.), *Employment Problems of Automation and Advanced Technology*. London: Macmillan: 304–17.

WHISLER, T. L. and SHULTZ, G. P. (1962). 'Automation and the Management Process', *The Annals of the American Academy of Political and Social Science*, No. 340: 81–90.

WHITEHEAD, T. N. (1936). *Leadership in a Free Society*. Cambridge, Mass.: Harvard University Press.

WHITEHILL, A. M., JR. (1964). 'Cultural Values and Employee Attitudes: United States and Japan', *Journal of Applied Psychology*, 48, 1: 69–72.

WHYTE, W. H. (1956). *The Organization Man*. New York: Simon & Schuster.

WHYTE, W. F. and WILLIAMS, L. K. (1963). 'Supervisory Leadership: An International Comparison', *Proceedings of CIOS XIII International Management Congress,* 26: 481–8.

WILENSKY, H. L. (1960). 'Work, Careers, and Social Integration', *International Social Science Journal,* XII, Fall: 543–60.

WILENSKY, H. (1963). 'The Moonlighter: A Product of Relative Deprivation', *Industrial Relations,* 3, 1, Oct.: 105–24.

WILENSKY, H. L. (1966). 'Work as a Social Problem', in H. S. BECKER (ed.), *Social Problems: A Modern Approach.* New York: Wiley: 138–42.

WILLENER, A. (1964). 'Payment Systems in the French Steel and Iron Mining Industry', in G. K. ZOLLSCHAN and W. HIRSCH (eds.), *Explorations in Social Change.* London: Routledge & Kegan Paul: 593–618.

WILLER, D. (1967). *Scientific Sociology.* Englewood Cliffs, N. J.: Prentice-Hall.

WILLIAMSON, O. E. (1964). *The Economics of Discretionary Behavior.* Englewood Cliffs, N.J.: Prentice-Hall.

WILSON, H. H. (1961). *Pressure Group.* London: Secker & Warburg.

WOODWARD, J. (1958). *Management and Technology.* London: H.M.S.O.

* WOODWARD, J. (1965). *Industrial Organization—Theory and Practice.* London: Oxford University Press. Explores relationships between the technology, administrative organization and economic performance of manufacturing companies. Conclusions based on twelve years of research utilizing both comparative survey and detailed case study methods.

WRAY, M. (1968). 'Business in a Capricious Environment', *Sunday Times,* 28th April: 36.

YOUNG, M. (1958). *The Rise of the Meritocracy 1870–2033.* London: Thames & Hudson.

YUCHTMAN, E. and SEASHORE, S. E. (1967). 'A System Resource Approach to Organizational Effectiveness', *American Sociological Review,* 32, 6, Dec.: 891–903.

ZALEWSKI, A. (1966). 'The Influence of Automation on Management', in J. STIEBER (ed.), *Employment Problems of Automation and Advanced Technology,* London: Macmillan: 354–67.

ZURCHER, L. A., MEADOW, A. and ZURCHER, S. L. (1965). 'Value Orientation, Role Conflict, and Alienation from Work: A Cross Cultural Study', *American Sociological Review,* 30, 4, Aug.: 539–48.

Subject Index